A SHOELEATHER HISTORY

of the

Wobblies

STORIES *of the* INDUSTRIAL
WORKERS OF THE WORLD
(IWW) *in* CONNECTICUT

by Steve Thornton

PUBLISHED BY:

The Shoeleather History Project

shoeleatherhistoryproject.com

2013

1ˢᵗ Edition

ISBN-13: 978-0-9898224-0-4

PRINTED BY:

Red Sun Press — proud members of UAW Local 1596

Boston, Massachusetts, USA

DESIGN BY:

Christian C Murray

Fonts: *FF Atma* by Alan Dague-Greene & *Dalliance Flourishes* by Frank Heine

For Kate, Matthew, Megan & Pepper

Contents

Introduction

Yes, the long memory is the most radical idea in this country.
— Utah Phillips

I study the past because I am interested in the future.
— Peter Rachleff

Storm Centers

On the morning of June 27, 1905, Bill Haywood used a piece of wood as a gavel to open the founding convention of the Industrial Workers of the World (IWW) in Chicago. Later that same day in Hartford Connecticut, the State Senate voted to build an Armory for the protection of businesses located in "storm centers for anticipated riots or strikes."

The timing was pure coincidence. The two events, however, signaled a coming collision. As Jeremy Brecher wrote in his labor history *Strike!* state governments built armories as fortresses in American cities "not against invasion from abroad but against popular revolt at home."

Certainly, Connecticut's lawmakers could not see into the future. They had no idea how threatened they would become by the IWW's organizing efforts throughout the state. Instead, the legislators made their case for the armory by invoking the great nationwide railroad strike of 1877, the recent labor unrest in Waterbury, and earlier union strikes right nearby on Capitol Avenue. Acting in the interest of local industrialists, the elected officials argued not *if* the armory should be built, but *where* it would do the most good. Some favored a location near the state house; others said it should be built near the Colt Firearms factory. A former Hartford mayor testified he wished he had the use of an armory to protect public order in 1901 when striking machinists took over Hartford's streets.

State Armory, Hartford, Conn.
72855

By 1919, the Connecticut General Assembly had approved funding for armories across the state and had passed laws designed to curb union organizing efforts. By that time the radical IWW was shaking the very foundations of the nation's economic system. And although the union officially shunned the political arena, the Wobblies threatened capitalism's hold on the electoral system as well, with battles in the workplace that spilled over into the voting booth, particularly in support of the Socialist Party presidential candidate Eugene Debs. Many Connecticut workers, poor, suffering, and powerless, would find the IWW's appeal to take control of their own destinies very compelling.

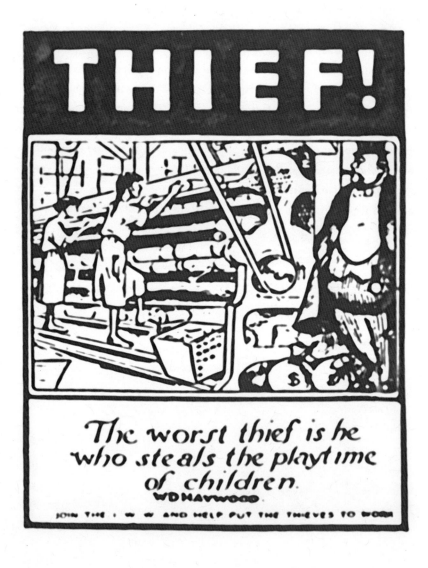

"More emphasis on property than on life"

At the turn of the 20th century, it was a dangerous proposition for a worker to join any union. You could be fired and no law existed to protect you. You could be blacklisted, and no other company would hire you. And worst of all, being a union supporter could get you beaten by employer-hired vigilantes, private detectives, the police, or even the military, as workers and organizers have discovered throughout American history. Retaliation was frequent from employers who feared losing control of their property, which meant workers as well as machines. Their prerogatives as captains of industry were also threatened. Why should they give up their wealth, status, leisure and power to a bunch of ragtag foreigners?

Here is what workers faced every day on the job in Connecticut—and around the country—during the first half of the 20th century:

The Blacklist: Companies quickly learned that union organizers, when identified by supervisors and fired, would move to another shop. The bosses maintained a list of workers they considered troublemakers and shared what they knew through their employer associations. The law was of no use to blacklisted workers. The state legislature banned company blacklists in 1911. The bosses objected and appealed. In 1912 the Connecticut Supreme Court upheld the lawmakers' ban. But that same year it was revealed that the Connecticut Manufacturers' Bureau kept tabs on discharged workers and communicated this information to businesses across the state. The list included the reasons for dismissal, including "wanted an undeserved increase" and "misunderstanding with the boss." Once on the blacklist, a worker found it impossible to find new employment. Scovill Manufacturing Company in Waterbury had a formidable spy system, as did Winchester Arms in New Haven. They both kept detailed files on every worker who seemed "suspicious."

Discrimination and Exploitation: Women, immigrant workers, children, and African Americans, who were just starting to become a significant part of the state's workforce, were ignored by the traditional labor unions. They had no representation and no power. These groups comprised a significant percentage of the working class, but they were rebuffed when they knocked on the door of the American Federation of Labor (AFL), the country's largest union coalition. They could not turn to the political system either: most of these workers didn't even have the right to vote. A study done by a special state commission in 1913 on the status of women workers found that most factories had no first aid resources even though accidents were epidemic. Toilets didn't work and changing rooms didn't exist. Connecticut working women totaled 49,000. More than 5,000 workers were minors. Almost 80% of the women were not married and supported themselves on wages that the commission said was "barely a living wage."

Long hours, poverty pay: The work day ranged from 10 to 16 hours for at least six days a week. Parents and their young children worked in the mills together. And still, for millions of unskilled workers, take-home pay barely fed most families. The Quidnick Mill in Willimantic was one example. Like Walmart workers today who must count on government-subsidized health care, the Quidnick workers in 1912 had to rely on public assistance even though entire families worked full time.

Deadly jobs: Matilda Cevitti worked at American Hatter and Furrier in Danbury. No effective state or federal laws required safety devices on factory machines. On April 6, 1906, Matilda was standing near a revolving machine shaft that generated static and caught her hair. The shaft ripped off her scalp and caused serious injuries to her face, hearing, and eyesight. "This is a great country for liberty, but we lay more emphasis on liberty of property than we do on liberty of life," declared a safety expert from Hartford-based Travelers Insurance Company. He reported that across the country, two million workers were injured each year and one hundred workers *a day* died from industrial accidents.

Speed ups: Always looking for methods to increase the pace of work and thereby increase profits, Connecticut employers such as the Yale & Towne Company utilized the "scientific management" method known as the Taylor system. Workers' smallest movements were carefully measured in order to eliminate delays and speed up production. It wasn't just efficiency the boss was after. Taylorism also had the effect of stealing the trade secrets that workers had developed to perform their jobs. By studying the work, the boss could appropriate a worker's techniques—actually, his property—and replace him with an unskilled worker or a machine. In 1912, Congressman John Q. Tilson of New Haven spoke out against Taylorism, citing a study that found it gave managers a "dangerously high level of uncontrolled power."

Poor housing: Living conditions were so bad in Hartford that a "sweeping investigation" was done in 1904, resulting in modest reforms. A decade later, little had changed: tenement apartments still had no running water or indoor toilets, insects infested the dwellings, garbage filled the yards and children died from the polluted water of the Park River (known as the Hog River because it was so polluted). Landlords easily got around the zoning laws, causing overcrowding which fostered the spread of diseases such as tuberculosis and diphtheria. A local minister complained that "industries are parasites and are taking lives from the country [local farms]," without creating adequate housing in the cities. Where industry did provide housing, like the Moosup textile mill, employers used it as leverage against union organizing. In March, 1906, the mill boss issued eight hundred eviction notices after the Moosup weavers went on strike.

Why would Connecticut workers join the IWW?

These conditions can certainly explain why workers would join a union to improve their conditions. But why the IWW? The Wobblies were condemned by clergymen, outlawed by politicians, lied about by the press and attacked by the police. Even the term "Wobbly," a nickname with an unclear origin, seemed strange.

There were two reasons workers were attracted to the IWW. First, unskilled workers were largely ignored by the traditional craft unions. The dominant voice of labor was the AFL and its president Sam Gompers, who ran the coalition for thirty-eight years. The federation was comprised of craft union members, skilled white males who jealously guarded their own benefits to the exclusion of all others. The IWW called the AFL the "American *Separation* of Labor" because the group could not even get its constituent unions to cooperate with each other against common employers.

Workers turned to the organization that had as its principle "one big union" of all working people. The IWW projected "a vision of a really democratic society," not one where plutocrats ruled the economy, according to historian Paul Buhle. "Decentralized democracy, democratic decision-making at all levels, is the most radical idea ever hatched in North America and the only one with real lasting appeal."

There was another reason the IWW attracted unorganized workers, less tangible but just as important. The Wobblies offered the workers a new labor culture, one that included them and respected their own languages and traditions. It was a culture that sang to them.

The Wobs had their own celebrities, brazen figures like Elizabeth Gurley Flynn who could mesmerize thousands at a mass rally. They had their own troubadours, like Joe Hill who lampooned hypocrites in high places and cut them down to size. The IWW had its own sound track, with scores of tunes sung from the "Little Red Songbook" that kept up workers' morale in dark times. The song *Solidarity Forever* is still sung at union meetings, even though many workers don't know it came from the Wobblies.

Immigrants didn't have to change their names and lose their accents to join the Wobblies. They were welcome to join as themselves, and the union adapted to *them* with newspapers in a dozen languages, interpreters at meetings, and organizers like Joe Ettor, who looked and dressed as if he could be a cousin who just landed at Ellis Island.

The Wobblies communicated through "silent agitators," small stickers with pithy ideas. They could boil down big concepts into highly potent weapons. *"An Injury to One is an Injury to All,"* they declared. *"We will build a new society within the shell of the old." "One Big Union for all workers."* IWW organizers were ready to sacrifice their comfort, safety, and their lives to make those slogans a reality.

The following stories tell the tale of what workers discovered in themselves when they joined the Wobblies, and how much they endured in order to become IWW members in Connecticut's mill and factory towns.

Despite the destruction of records from police raids and internal splits, much of the IWW's history has been documented. Still, very little research on Wobbly organizing has been done in Connecticut. According to the Hartford Trade Board, Hartford had "wholly escaped the contagion [of] any rash agitator who should attempt to disturb the harmony" of the city. Historians have quoted this business group's glib assurance as proof of labor peace, but the record tells a different tale.

PROLOGUE: *Forerunners*

Before the birth of the IWW, there were organizers and visionaries sowing the seeds for a new type of union, and a new society as well. One such organization was the Knights of Labor which was particularly active in Connecticut. At their peak in the 1880s, this combination of local unions had 12,000 state members in 62 towns around Connecticut. While the Knights attempted some local workplace organizing, they found their greatest success in the political arena. In 1885 the Connecticut General Assembly could boast as many as 37 elected Knights who successfully passed laws limiting child labor and protecting worker health and safety. The Knights believed in the industrial model of organizing, all workers with the same boss in one union, as opposed to craft unionism which pitted groups of workers against each other.

Two of the famous figures who would later play key roles in the IWW visited the state and planted their vision of a revolutionary future. Lucy Parsons and James Connolly came from different parts of the world, but they both ended up inspiring working men and women in Connecticut and across the country.

Get Mrs. Parsons to Stop Talking

Lucy Parsons was met at New Haven's Union Station by a group of "anarchists and cigar makers," according to a press report. It was October 30, 1886, and Parsons was on a two-month speaking tour in support of her husband, who had just been sentenced to death.

Albert Parsons and seven other men had been convicted of inciting the "Haymarket riot," a massive peaceful demonstration in Chicago just five months earlier on May 4th. Striking workers were in Haymarket Square, demanding the eight-hour day and an end to police repression, when a bomb exploded in the crowd, killing several police officers. The police fired indiscriminately, killing and injuring many innocent workers. To this day no one knows for certain who caused the explosion, but Parsons and most of his compatriots were hanged for it. The labor movement was dealt a serious blow.

Lucy Parsons addressed an enthusiastic crowd at New Haven's Lincoln Rink on Saturday night. She spoke for more than ninety minutes to 200 people, mostly German and Polish workers. A number of Yale students attended as well. She talked about the Haymarket trial, which had been covered in all the state's newspapers. Parsons urged the abolition of the wage system and of government as well. "Nature made all the laws man needs" she proclaimed. Two police detectives were in the audience, and when one of them got up to leave, the crowd booed him.

"You may have expected me to belch forth great flames of dynamite and stand before you with bombs in my hands," the speaker told the crowd. "If you are disappointed, you have only the capitalist press to thank for it."

On that same tour Parsons spoke to an even bigger crowd in Bridgeport. According to historian Carolyn Asbaugh's biography, *Lucy Parsons, American Revolutionary,* the activist was thrilled by the eagerness of the audience's interest in anarchism. "My trip is having its effect," she wrote Albert. "The powers that be don't know what to do with me. One New York paper suggests that Albert Parsons 'be let out as a compromise to get Mrs. Parsons to stop talking.'"

Although their execution was delayed for a year due to the intense support campaign generated by Parsons and others, the Haymarket martyrs were hanged on November 11, 1887. Her work, however, was far from over. In 1905 she was back in Chicago, on the platform with Big Bill Haywood, ushering in the birth of the Industrial Workers of the World. Lucy Parsons remained an organizer until her death in 1942.

Living by a Battle Plan

It was a fall day in 1902 when the Irishman arrived in Hartford. He came to organize Americans into the one big union. James Connolly spent his life as a street corner speaker, newspaper editor, revolutionary theoretician and a tireless organizer. He believed strongly in the IWW, and ultimately died a martyr supporting the creation of an Irish Republic and the end of British colonial rule.

Connolly visited the U.S. first on a tour under the auspices of the Socialist Labor Party (SLP). His personal finances were so poor that he had to rely on friends to provide him with a respectable suit to wear. According to his biographer Samuel Levenson, "Connolly had little interest in making a living; his goal was to liberate the working class. He lived by a battle plan."

The purpose of Connolly's trip was to "enlist the interest of Irish Americans in the socialist movement" and convince them that voting for socialist candidates was not contrary to their national or religious heritage.

The Irish organizer's speaking tour lasted four months. One of his first stops was Germania Hall in Hartford on September 24, 1902. The hall was built to serve the needs of the city's German population but it was frequently used by many local unions and ethnic groups. By the turn of the century, the Irish were Hartford's largest ethnic population.

There appears to be no written record of Connolly's Hartford speech, which was entitled "Home Rule and Socialism." But he wrote about the same subject in the Irish newspaper *Workers' Republic*. "Home rule" was the dominant movement for Irish independence at the time, run by the Irish upper class. "We are out for Ireland for the Irish," Connolly explained. "But who are the Irish? Not the rack-renting, slum-owning landlord; not the sweating, profit-grinding capitalist... The cause of labour is the cause of Ireland and the cause of Ireland is the cause of labour. They cannot be dissevered."

Was Hartford ready for James Connolly's vision of a new political and economic order? In April, the city had elected Ignatius A. Sullivan as mayor on the third party "Economic League" ticket. Sullivan was a union man who had worked in a paper mill as a ten-year old boy. He joined the Knights of Labor and became a union organizer for the retail clerks. He helped settle a Hartford machinists' strike that achieved the nine-hour day. Sullivan's election was seen as a significant victory for Hartford's working class. It is not known if he and Connolly met during the latter's brief stop in the city, but it seems likely that the new mayor was in the audience with hundreds of other Hartfordites when Connolly spoke.

James Connolly was a dedicated revolutionary, but he still had to make a living and support his family. The impoverished organizer briefly tried his hand as an insurance salesman in Troy, New York, but his time there coincided with a shirt factory strike and he ended up collecting funds for striking workers instead of insurance premiums. Right after that, Connolly applied for a job with the Connecticut branch of the Socialist Labor Party (SLP), but the offer fell through. He later broke with the SLP largely because of party leader Daniel De Leon's dictatorial style and sectarian policies; De Leon responded that Connolly was a "police spy."

Connolly welcomed the 1905 birth of the IWW in Chicago. He raised funds in 1906 to defend Bill Haywood while he was on trial in Idaho and became an IWW organizer in 1907. On behalf of the Wobblies, the Irishman organized trolley car workers, garment workers, milkmen and dock workers. He became close friends with Elizabeth Gurley Flynn, the young Irish American activist who was also an IWW organizer.

He returned to Ireland in 1910. Connolly signed the 1916 Proclamation that set out the principles of true Irish independence and sparked a short-lived rebellion against the British empire. As the commander of the Irish Citizen Army, he was wounded during the doomed Easter Rising. When the revolt failed, Connolly was captured by British forces, imprisoned at Kilmainham Jail and executed on May 12th. His wounds were so serious he had to be strapped to a chair in order to face the firing squad.

James Connolly once said that "if I don't die fighting for Ireland, I'll leave behind people who will."

Freedom to speak & sing

*Singing and working and fighting are so close you can't hardly tell
where one quits and the other begins.*
— *Woody Guthrie*

*Let there be a 'free speech fight' on in some town, and the 'wobblies' converge
upon it, across a thousand miles, and fill the jails with champions. And singing.
Remember, this is the only American working class movement which sings.*
—*John Reed*

FREEDOM TO SPEAK & SING ———————

Free Speech in America? It didn't exist for working people in the early 1900's. Until workers and their unions fought for it—in the courts and in the streets—the First Amendment was an illusion for Connecticut's working people.

In 1791, a sufficient number of states approved the Bill of Rights, which guaranteed that Congress could not infringe on freedom of speech or freedom of assembly. Connecticut was not among those states voting in favor at the time. In practice, however, ordinary people could not speak on public property unless they won explicit permission from local authorities, whose right to limit rallies or speeches was affirmed by a Supreme Court ruling in 1897 (Davis v. Commonwealth of Massachusetts). When a minister preached on Boston Common and was arrested, the justices wrote that the First Amendment "does not have the effect of creating a particular and personal right in the citizen to use public property in defiance of the Constitution and laws of the state."

Over the next four decades, local soap-boxers suffered the consequences of that decision. In 1904, union organizers were arrested for violating Torrington's "hand-bill law" when they distributed leaflets. In 1912, socialist Cornelius Foley tried to speak to downtown Hartford crowds but was denied permission. The police forced him to a run-down corner where hustlers hawked medical cures. In 1914 another socialist began to "jawbone" in front of Parson's Theater but was interrupted by a police officer who charged him with breach of peace for speaking in public without a license.

Between 1907 and 1916, Wobblies mounted spectacular campaigns in the U.S. and Canada to liberate the public square. In order to spread the union gospel, organizers had to battle big businesses, police, city councils and courts, all of which colluded to silence the IWW. More often than not, the Wobblies won, sometimes at a very high price.

First Stirrings

Just a few months after the IWW concluded its 1905 founding convention, the union's organizers were in Hartford. At an open air meeting on the corner of Park and Broad Streets, James Lee and Joe Campbell addressed a large crowd on Friday evening, September 15, 1905.

Lee had reason to support "one big union." As an executive board member of the Amalgamated Association of Street and Electric Railway Employees, he was part of a massive strike that began on March 7th, halting New York City's elevated railways. The streetcar workers were joined by the local Brotherhood of Locomotive Engineers, but the engineers' national leaders quickly disowned the job action, fatally weakening the strike. "The American Federation of Labor is not controlled by labor men," Lee told the crowd, "but by the capitalists and trusts."

Joe Campbell, a member of the Socialist Labor Party from Philadelphia, declared that "concerted action... is the only way to get results." Campbell went on to explain that the IWW was about more than getting just another nickel. "We do not spend our time advocating an eight-hour law and two per cent increase in wages," he said. "That is getting only crumbs thrown out by the capitalists." His words were a direct challenge to the dominant idea that, at best, unions could only shorten their hours and increase their wages by a few pennies.

In fact, the Wobblies *did* end up taking on fights for immediate improvements in Connecticut factories. But as historian Melvyn Dubofsky has pointed out, while the union struggled for short-term gains, they insisted that "reform and revolution need not be mutually exclusive... the Wobblies always sought tomorrow's utopia."

In his comments on a typesetters' strike that had just taken place in Hartford, Campbell made the IWW's strategy clear: "If the plan of the Industrial Workers of the World were carried out you would not see a few compositors striking in this city. The demands of the few would be backed up by pressmen, elevator boys and everyone connected with the business. All trades would work together in the same way for a common end, and with all united in common cause, their rights could not be withheld."

The Streets Belong to the People

The fight for free speech has been part of the Wobblies' lasting legacy. For the union it was a practical matter: in order to spur workers into action, you had to be able to talk with large numbers of them at the same time. Despite the fact that there were many labor newspapers, the big dailies were run by the monied interests. The boss owned the factory floor. Street corner speaking, then, was the logical option.

Hartford trade unionists had already discovered the obstacles to free speech. The Amalgamated Trades Union wanted to use Bushnell Park for a mass meeting in 1884 but the mayor denied them permission. The Board of Aldermen overruled the mayor. "The general argument was that the park belonged to the people," the *Hartford Courant* reported. Labor won that battle, but there were many more to come.

The IWW faced constant challenges in its ability to spread the word. Up and down the West Coast thousands of IWW members got themselves arrested and filled the jails in order to force local governments to allow them to speak. According to historian Philip Foner, the first IWW free speech fight took place in Toronto in 1906. Not much is known about this incident other than the fact that the local police stopped Wobblies from street-corner speaking and the matter went to court. Across the U.S., free-speech Wobblies suffered beatings, severe hardships, terrible jail conditions and sometimes death. Manufacturers created vigilante groups to kidnap, imprison, torture and deport workers, but in almost every case the free speech campaigns eventually won out.

Just a few months after the IWW was born, a lone Wobbly organizer staged his own free speech fight in Connecticut.

In August, 1905 machinist Joseph P. Campbell moved from Philadelphia and became the IWW's first Connecticut organizer. He was sponsored by the local Socialist Labor Party (SLP) with its office on 2 State Street in Hartford. Although the SLP split with the IWW in 1908 and set up a rival group, this political party initially worked within the Wobbly organization for the common goal of building a revolutionary industrial union.

Even though he was just 25 years old, Campbell had already engaged in "soapbox" speaking for several years. He had been involved in a Pennsylvania coal miners' strike where he was run out of town and threatened with death if he returned. Later, the SLP supported his successful court challenge to a Philadelphia ban on public speaking. Now Campbell was ready to test whether or not free speech existed in the self-proclaimed Constitution state.

In early September Joe Campbell and James Lee had organized open air meetings twice in Hartford: once at Park and Broad Streets and the next night downtown on the corner of Trumbull and Asylum. There was no report of police disruption at either meeting, both of which were apparently well attended.

On September 29, 1905 Joe was in Meriden, the manufacturing home of silver, cutlery, and firearms. The Court Street square in the center of town was the perfect site for the Wobbly's purpose. Campbell walked to the police station and informed Chief George Van Nostrand he would be speaking on Friday and Saturday. The organizer requested that two policemen to be assigned to the event. The chief informed him that a permit from the mayor was required. As Campbell described it, "I told the chief that this was not Russia, that it was America and we didn't have to have permits here to speak."

More than 500 people crowded the square as Campbell set up his dry goods box on the street corner, a short distance from the town's fountain. "Campbell was the magnet that drew," confirmed one police officer. Chief Van Nostrand and his men were watching as Joe spoke, "gesturing and bellowing" to the crowd. After about ten minutes a police captain approached the speaker. The captain reported that Joe paused to ask his name and then said he would "roast" the cop. Instead he kept his focus on his speech, compared the U.S. to czarist Russia, and was soon arrested. The crowd followed the prisoner and the police to the Colony Street police station. After a night in jail, the young Wobbly was bailed out by an SLP official.

Four days later at the Meriden police court, Joe Campbell faced charges of breach of the peace and obstruction. Since he was not accused of failing to obtain a speaking permit, it seems clear the authorities were trying to avoid a constitutional fight. Instead the prosecutor simply argued that the Wobbly's speech impeded traffic. Campbell's lawyer countered that the Salvation Army frequently held open air meetings without police interference. Judge Fay found Joe Campbell guilty and fined him ten dollars. The judge proclaimed that "the streets do not belong to the unorganized public."

Taking It to the Street

On May 13, 1912, Wobbly organizers called their meeting to order on Main Street in Willimantic, known as the "Thread City." The event was in clear defiance of the city's chief of police, who had forbidden the public gathering because, he said, officials were afraid there might be a fight between IWW members and the rival United Textile Workers union. The chief told the Wobs to hire a hall instead. At least three hundred workers gathered anyway, listening to speakers until cops broke the meeting up, with people scattering in all directions. The heavy-handed police action only stimulated the Wobblies' desire to test the promise of free speech guaranteed by the Bill of Rights.

The IWW threatened to fill the Willimantic jails to win the right to speak. Wobbly organizer J.T. Bienkowski declared that fifty activists would stand at every street corner of the city "in open battle for the right of free speech." Bienkowski asserted that the police department would not succeed in denying the IWW's rights.

Wobblies had already engaged in five years of free speech fights across the country. These campaigns were a unique "direct action" strategy for educating workers on the class struggle. Rather than relying on courts or politicians to guarantee their freedoms, workers acted on their own behalf to immediately win their demands. Direct action was a practical necessity to counter the attempts of police, business and the AFL to oppose IWW organizing. At the same time a free speech fight in San Diego was raging, the IWW initiated a similar challenge in the Thread City. The Wobblies had recently won a strike of 1500 mill operators—Polish, French-Canadian, Syrian, and native born—at the American Thread Company in Willimantic. By May, the union was establishing a permanent local and a regional organizing office.

At one point, according to a press report, the union planned to stage a "test open air meeting" in the city. If they couldn't speak in the streets, they threatened, the Wobs would erect a large tent and hold a meeting there. In the end, the IWW called the city's bluff. By August 6th the union held a mass meeting at Lincoln Square on Main Street with no police interference. More than 500 workers assembled to hear Wobbly organizer Ben Legere, who spoke to the crowd for an hour and twenty minutes about the principles and goals of the Industrial Workers of the World.

Fellow Workers and Friends!

On a hot August day, Frederick Cederholm and IWW organizer Louis Nelson stood at the Bridgeport factory gate. They were at the Locomobile auto plant, preparing to address workers on their lunch hour. The police had other ideas. Before the meeting could start, the cops broke it up. Across the country, the IWW had won a well-deserved reputation for defending free speech, but in Bridgeport the fight had just begun.

Fred Cederholm was a local labor activist and a former city alderman, the first man to run and win on the Socialist ticket. It was not in his nature to give up easily. After the police rebuffed him, Cederholm met with the Mayor and got permission to speak at the factory the next day. The labor man addressed 400 workers at the gate and many more who were listening from the plant's windows. Cederholm asserted that the new "profit-sharing" plan the company was offering was a sucker's deal. Workers at Locomobile deserved the eight-hour day and nothing less, he said. Just down the street, Bullard Company workers had won a shorter workday—eight hours work for ten hours pay. Why shouldn't Locomobile workers get the same? The eight-hour demand signaled a "day already dawning for labor in Bridgeport," Cederholm declared.

One machinist provided the speaker with a soapbox. "Nobody can stop me from talking," Cederholm told the crowd. "I have become a citizen of this country and know the struggle for liberty upon which the United States was founded!"

Locomobile workers were on the move, Cederholm said. The Manufacturers' Association couldn't stop them; blacklists and firings would not deter their cause. "A grievance of one should be the grievance of all!" Cederholm proclaimed, quoting the IWW slogan. The workers broke into applause. Three policemen stood by and watched the speaker as it started to rain. The workers didn't leave; they gathered under a big tree for shelter and stayed to listen.

Mayor Wilson had allowed Cederholm to speak as a personal favor, but the city official was determined not to allow "agitators and disturbers" to roam about freely, spreading their dangerous ideas. The Mayor meant Louis Nelson, the Wobbly activist who had already been fired by Locomobile for union organizing. Known as an eloquent speaker, Nelson was 30 years old and had emigrated from Russia.

A vacant lot located at the end of South Main Street was secured a few days later so Nelson and the others could once again rally the Locomobile workers. The lot was right near the factory's testing area, but it was on private property.

As the speakers approached the site, the police stopped Nelson and told him he would not be allowed to conduct a meeting. "This is a free country," Nelson replied, "and we propose to speak." This time, 600 men and women workers were waiting. George Bowen of the Machinists union climbed onto a packing box and started the meeting. He was quickly arrested by police, who said they were acting under the Mayor's direct orders.

Without hesitation, Louis Nelson took Bowen's place. As one account put it, "his black raven locks were flowing in the wind, a peaked black felt hat was waving in his hand and with flashing eyes he announced 'As citizens of the United States we have the right of free speech. We are going to make addresses!'." The crowd exploded, drowning out the rest of his words as the cops took him away. "Stand by the eight hour day!" Nelson yelled over the noise.

Then Cederholm mounted the box. A cop warned him that he, too, would be arrested if he spoke. "I have not said a word yet," Cederholm replied. Then, turning to the crowd, he began: "Fellow Workers and friends!" The police dragged him off the crate as he continued to talk. Soon all three men were in custody and being driven off to jail. "Don't forget the eight hours, boys!" Cederholm yelled out the police wagon window as the crowd cheered. The soap

Birdseye View East Bridgeport, looking North East.

boxers passed by Bullard Company and kept up their agitation to those workers as well. Said one observer at the scene: "We talk about eight hours and the mayor orders our arrest. He only works two hours a day!"

All three men were charged with breach of the peace. Bond was initially set at $1,000 each (about $18,000 today). Eventually the bond was dropped for Cederholm and Bowen, but not for Nelson. Factory officials had made their displeasure known to the Mayor regarding the Wobbly. Radicals had been gathering at a "colony" in nearby Milford on Walnut Beach. Even the popular Joe Ettor had been staying there.

At the organizers' trial the next day, more than 100 workers attempted to enter the courtroom. Only one made it, and he was quickly ejected. The prosecutor argued that the Wobbly Louis Nelson had traveled from state to state under different aliases. The judge ruled this information irrelevant. The defense asked the police chief if he would have arrested the men had they been talking about religion or politics. The chief admitted he would not. The judge found the three men guilty, fined them each one dollar, and suspended their sentences..

The Locomobile Company had been building autos in Bridgeport for over thirty years. The plant's owner, S.T. Davis, could not understand why his 3000 employees were so eager to hear from the labor men. Didn't the workers prefer the bonus system Davis was offering instead of the eight-hour day? His foremen assured Davis that he was correct. The fact was, however, that the company men had been aggressively promoting the profit-sharing plan to the strikers' wives by distributing literature that criticized the shorter work week. This propaganda effort only made the Locomobile workers angrier.

The actions of the Mayor and the police produced widespread condemnation. *The Bridgeport Evening Farmer* called the arrests a "kidnapping" and editorialized that the Mayor's action was a "high-handed outrage." The paper declared "Standard Oil agents come and go, but Mayor Wilson never dreamed of denying the city to these out-of-town agitators." The Bridgeport Central Labor Union protested Wilson's actions as a threat to free speech and assembly, and asked the Board of Aldermen to consider impeachment (the aldermen buried the request in committee). A meeting of Hartford unionists offered their support to the embattled Bridgeport workers.

The arrests did not interrupt the workers' interest or their efforts to mobilize. Indeed, the factory gates were alive with debate—and not a cop in sight. On Saturday evening, the Locomobile workers held a mass meeting to discuss the possibility of going on strike. The company retaliated, firing 25 employees on

August 11th. Workers were sure that private detectives had been hired by the boss to act as spies on the factory floor.

The workers responded to the firings with another mass meeting on August 12th. Once again, Louis Nelson joined Fred Cederholm on the speakers' platform. Instead of starting with a rousing speech, the two men announced that a written message had just been received from Locomobile: owner Davis had just agreed to the eight-hour day!

"I know that the company does not like people such as myself and brother Cederholm," Louis Nelson triumphantly told the assembly. "But in some way I am proud of that fact. I am glad to be termed an agitator when I can go into a factory where people are working 10 to 20 hours [a day] and through my discharge benefit them all. When a policeman pats me on the back and tells me I am a pretty good fellow, I think something is wrong with me."

The next day, the Manufacturers' Association announced that all plants in Bridgeport would move to the nine-hour day as a compromise. Thirteen hundred young women at the Warner Brothers corset factory were not satisfied with this half measure. Emboldened by the Locomobile workers, they responded by going out on strike. George Bowen met with Mayor Wilson, who was described as "unsettled and uncertain" when Bowen told him there would be more public agitation if Bridgeport's employers refused to accede to the workers' demand for an eight-hour day.

Mayor Wilson spoke at the New Haven Labor Day rally a few weeks after the arrests. He was positioning himself for statewide office by soliciting support of union workers. He succeeded-- Wilson was elected Lieutenant Governor in the fall. Criticism still dogged him, so Wilson tried to blame his anti-labor actions on Louis Nelson. Workers didn't need "the aid of any IWW agitators," he explained. "Nelson said he would make Bridgeport another Lawrence, another Paterson," the Mayor pleaded. "He is the man who is the close personal friend of Ettor. The one necessary to keep quiet was this man Nelson," he cried, as if he was trying to convince himself.

Three days later, a parade of black cats marched down Bridgeport's Main Street. The Black Cat had become a powerful IWW symbol. Also known as the "Sabcat" for sabotage, it indicated a Wobbly presence ready to take action. The animals streaming through downtown, however, weren't the One Big Feline Union, just a publicity stunt organized by a local clothing store. But who knows what the "unsettled and uncertain" Mayor Wilson thought?

Songs to Fan the Flames

Steve Kaminsky sang Wobbly songs all the way to the Waterbury jail. It was Wednesday, March 9, 1919; Kaminsky and 200 other workers had just been arrested on a raid of the IWW's Bank Street hall. The rowdy crowd kept up their singing in the jail throughout the night.

The cops confiscated literature written in Russian, Italian and English, along with the charters for the Waterbury and New Haven IWW locals, and the Wobblies' Little Red Songbook, subtitled "Songs to Fan the Flames of Discontent." The arrests were triggered by federal agents who had been spying on local workers' meetings for several weeks.

While most of the men arrested were soon freed, the police kept ten leaders in jail, including the 28-year old Russian Steve Kaminsky who had been organizing brass mill workers in the city for the past two years. Also detained were Alexander Chernoff, a national organizer for the IWW, New England organizers Sam Bernow (probably Hartford's Sam Bernowsky) and Mark Zeitlin, and two local union officers, Paul Matecky and Alex Pashug.

After a three-day trial, Chernoff, Bernow and Zeitlin were given six-month jail sentences for unlawful assembly. Steve Kaminsky was found guilty as well, but he was put on six-months' probation.

The Waterbury case was held up as an example on how other cities should deal with the IWW's presence. Three days after the Waterbury raid, 200 more Wobblies were arrested in New York.

Brass manufacturers, including the Scovill company, blamed "irresponsible agitators of the IWW and anarchistic types" for the continuing labor agitation. By June 18th the work of Steve Kaminsky and others was producing results. In Ansonia, Derby and Waterbury, more than 6000 brass mill workers struck for higher pay and shorter hours.

The workers' vehicle was the Waterbury Workers Association, a grassroots effort that organized along industrial lines and ethnic groupings as the IWW did. It rejected the American Federation of Labor's overtures. The AFL had ignored low-wage Waterbury workers for years, and the belated appearance of state federation head J.M. Orburn did not impress the strikers.

Over the course of a week, more and more shops were shut down. Mass meetings of thousands of strikers were held. At one point workers faced cops in a pitched battle where many were injured. Police and City Guards patrolled the streets with machine guns. Three special deputies (one Russian and two Lithuanians) resigned in protest of the harsh treatment of strikers.

Federal agents were engaged in uncovering the "real" strike leaders, convinced that the local spokesmen were only figureheads. The feds believed that the New York IWW was directing the action in Waterbury.

A 24-member committee emerged to negotiate with the employers. Steve Kaminsky was a member, and he also served on a three-man team that worked to negotiate peace with the city. At one point Kaminsky addressed four thousand strikers at an outdoor meeting. Observers, including the police, considered him the strike's most impressive speaker, with a powerful voice that reached the entire crowd.

Nine days into the strike, Steve Kaminsky was arrested. His room was searched and the police said they found IWW literature. Apparently, federal agents had identified him as a traveling organizer for the Wobblies. Still on probation from the March raid on the IWW headquarters, Kaminsky was forced to leave the state or face a stiff jail term.

Soon enough, thousands of workers won 10 to 25% wage increases and overtime pay, but still no union recognition. The Waterbury Workers Association and the AFL both continued recruiting.

Just before the strike had begun, a newspaper account related the defiant words of an unnamed young, well-spoken Russian worker: "If we are not permitted to hold meetings in the halls, we will hold them on the green … We will meet because the Constitution gives us the right to meet." To meet, and to sing.

Like an Oak Tree

Carlo Tresca stepped onto the stage at Waterbury's Concordia Hall, preparing to read from the Connecticut State Constitution. The police informed the Italian anarchist he would be arrested if he spoke. Tresca had been prevented from appearing in Waterbury once already, and he was back again. In front of the crowd that had come to see him, he demanded to be taken in by the police. The police refused.

In 1923, the Bureau of Investigation (known later as the FBI) made sure that Waterbury police understood that this man Tresca posed a danger to law and order. The Bureau had been keeping tabs on him for at least five years. Tresca had been an activist since his arrival from Italy in 1904, and an IWW supporter since he spoke to Italian workers in Bridgeport during the 1907 AT&S strike.

Carlo Tresca was a tireless anti-fascist, speaking and organizing against Benito Mussolini's regime. He edited a number of newspapers, including *Il Martello* (The Hammer), covering labor and anarchist campaigns. It was Tresca who led a march in Lawrence, Massachusetts of 10,000 strikers in defiance of a police ban against public demonstrations. Tresca organized workers during the IWW's 1916 Mesabi iron range strike in Minnesota where he was charged with inciting to riot (the charges were dropped). He worked to halt the executions of Joe Hill and Sacco and Vanzetti. He organized silk workers in Paterson, New Jersey, hotel workers, barbers and the unemployed in New York City.

According to Tresca's FBI file released under the Freedom of Information Act, Agent William Loughran traveled from Hartford to the Waterbury Police headquarters on the morning of February 25, 1923. Tresca was scheduled to give a talk in the city; he had appeared in years past without police interference. At the Sunday morning meeting, however police Superintendent George Beach decided that Tresca would not be allowed to speak. Beach assigned twenty police officers and detectives to the job, leaving the rest of the city virtually unprotected. The cops broke up the gathering before it could begin. Police did nothing to stop a pro-fascist meeting from taking place later that day with about 400 people, though, presumably because it was located at Our Lady of Lourdes church.

After the February standoff, Tresca promised that he would be back. Superintendent Beach wrote to the Department of Justice to help stop the anarchist's next appearance. The response from the Bureau was a "strictly confidential" record of Tresca's organizing efforts and the many attempts—all unsuccessful—by various government bodies to convict him on charges of sedition and incitement to riot.

Five hundred people packed the hall on Sunday afternoon, March 11th. On stage with Tresca was Roger Nash Baldwin. Roger was a child of the privileged class, and yet during World War I he deliberately violated the Selective Service Act and was sentenced to prison. In 1919 Baldwin joined the IWW and found work as a laborer. Around this same period he took on the cause of protecting the civil liberties of Wobblies and others who were the target of government repression. The American Civil Liberties Union, which Baldwin had founded, criticized Beach and attempted to break the police ban.

This time Tresca was armed with a copy of Connecticut's constitution. The idea to read it on stage came from Rabbi Lewis Browne of the city's Temple Israel, who sympathized with Tresca's efforts and suggested that reading the document in public would put the ban to the test.

Not even the presence of Baldwin and another ACLU member, Rev. Frederick Lauderburn of the Berkeley Divinity School, was sufficient to win Tresca the right to speak. An editorial writer from the *Waterbury Republican* questioned whether or not "the state constitution applies in Waterbury." To emphasize the point, the newspaper reprinted on its front page the sections of the constitution that guaranteed freedom of speech and assembly.

Tresca made a final attempt to address his Brass City supporters on March 25th. The police were again out in full force, this time equipped with riot guns. Tresca was not even allowed in the hall, although other activists spoke in English and Italian from the stage against fascism and for the First Amendment.

The federal government was not finished with Carlo Tresca. Soon after his Waterbury appearances, he was indicted for sending obscene material through the mail. The evidence? A two-line advertisement in *Il Martello* for a birth control book. The government had confiscated all copies of the newspaper, however, so subscribers never even saw it. Tresca eventually spent four months in federal prison until public pressure forced Calvin Coolidge to commute his sentence. The feds also worked hard to deport Tresca based on his legal status. Part of their evidence came from a Waterbury newspaper reporter. The newspaper man, at

the behest of a federal agent, asked Tresca if he was an American citizen. Tresca supposedly admitted that he was not.

While Carlo Tresca was routinely barred from public speaking events in the state, he sometimes got lucky. In 1917 he had been involved in an anarchist labor theatre troupe that performed in New Britain. On November 2, 1919, Tresca spoke in Hartford at the Princess Theater. According to a confidential federal report, the meeting was organized by Girolomo Grasso of 150 Market Street. On Tresca's agenda was the recent "annexation" of the Yugoslavian port city of Fiume by Italian fascists. Three hundred people listened to his speech.

Tresca has been credited with helping to keep Benito Mussolini's influence from fully taking hold in Italian-American communities during the 20s and 30s. He was constantly subjected to physical attacks from fascists, repeatedly harassed by the government, and more than once the target of assassination. Carlo Tresca was murdered on a New York street in 1943, most likely on Mussolini's orders.

Carlo Tresca always knew where he stood. "I continue to remain on this side of the barricade, like an oak tree," he wrote, "against god and master."

N.Y. —LAWRENCE STRIKE MEETING

Victories & Defeats

> You never lose a strike. You frighten the robbers and
> arm yourselves and your brothers.
> — *Mother Jones*

> The struggle is eternal. The tribe increases. Somebody else carries on.
> — *Ella Baker*

VICTORIES & DEFEATS ────

The history of the IWW, and in fact, of all fights for social justice, is full of important victories and crushing failures. Each gain, once achieved, must be constantly defended. Every loss can teach us the extent, and limits, of our collective power. Even failures warn the boss not to underestimate us. Union organizers know this, and nobody knew it better than the Wobblies. Their movement stood in stark contrast to the AFL leaders who ignored the hard work of organizing the unorganized and instead hob-nobbed with businessmen and copied their lavish lifestyles.

The specific campaigns in this chapter are not well known. Many have not been recorded before, nor are they part of labor's oral tradition. But all of these struggles deserve to be remembered, and learned from.

Rolling Thunder in Bridgeport

Frank Zambor was a stool pigeon. As a loyal employee at American Tube & Stamping Company (AT&S), Zambor spied for the boss and reported on his co-workers' union organizing activities. The workers discovered his treachery, so the boss had Zambor locked up in the Bridgeport police station for his own protection. The next morning—May 18, 1907-- he was safely placed on a train headed for New York.

Bridgeport's factories were ripe for IWW organizing, which may be why employers resorted to surveillance and strong arm tactics against the city's industrial workers. AFL head Sam Gompers had just written an article on May 1st that appeared in the *Bridgeport Post* entitled "Labor Enjoying Great Prosperity." But he wasn't talking about Bridgeport's immigrant workforce. Most working families were barely getting by in the city that one historian called an "industrial fortress."

The IWW's first efforts in Bridgeport can be traced to a 1907 strike of about 100 machinists on May 18th. These skilled tradesmen, members of the AFL's Machinists union, demanded a 54-hour week. They achieved it by simply stopping their machines on Saturday morning at 11:00 a.m. They left the factory by climbing over the locked gate, taking the company by surprise and quickly winning their demands. What made this action so unusual, and successful, was the support from unskilled AT&S workers, some of whom walked out with the machinists. These lower-paid workers were IWW sympathizers.

That same day in Chicago the IWW was considering a request by Bridgeport activists for increased support. Within a month, organizer Samuel French, fresh from an IWW strike at the Marston Woolen Mills in Maine, was in town to organize IWW Metal and Machinery Workers Union Local 113. His work was noted by local newspapers including the sympathetic *Bridgeport Evening Farmer*, which listed the IWW's local storefront headquarters at 477 Main Street near Railroad Avenue. French focused on the Hungarian workforce, the city's largest immigrant group and the majority of the AT&S workers. He was assisted by Louis Basky, a Hungarian-speaking Wobbly from Philadelphia.

American Tube & Stamping made steel parts for stoves, sewing machines, typewriters and many other goods. The company's hot mills on Howard Avenue produced sheet metal. On Hancock Street, the cold mills strengthened and hardened the steel. Both functions took place on the city's west side where the Hungarian community lived. On the east side, Stratford Avenue was the site of the company's billet mills where the metal took its final shape, ready for manufacturing use.

On July 16th, two months after the machinists' strike, workers at the AT&S west side plants walked off the job in response to management's decision to end their rotating shifts. The old schedule had allowed workers to alternate between day and evening hours. When the change was announced, forty workers acted as couriers to spread the bad news throughout the plant. A committee of six workers—three machinists and three laborers—went to boss Frank Wilmot to express their anger and deliver their demands. The workers wanted their rotation shifts restored, raises for all employees, higher pay for night shift workers, and union recognition. Wilmot, who had inherited the business from his father, passed the buck to his board of directors. They would not be meeting for another week.

On the first day of the strike, hundreds of AT&S strikers mingled outside the plants with other area factory workers including those employed by the American Graphophone company. Rumors spread that a general strike of all the city's workers was imminent. The Wobblies immediately reached out to the local Machinists union, since most of the machinists had walked off the job at AT&S as well. Within two days, the west side plants had shut down. Wilmot

responded that the company would close the mill and consolidate it with his east side works. In response, Sam French told reporters "we are determined to stand for our rights, for we consider that we are asking for nothing more than we are absolutely entitled to obtain."

Each morning, hundreds of workers conducted "silent parades" through Bridgeport streets. The strikers were not used to being the focus of public attention, but these immigrants in their rough work clothes soon became bolder as well-dressed businessmen scurried to avoid them.

Company owner Wilmot countered the strike's growing momentum by having his wife distribute leaflets offering $1000 to strikers' children if their fathers would return to work. This carrot came with a stick: the boss threatened to permanently replace anyone who stayed off the job. Strikers responded by burning the leaflets in a bonfire. Pressure also came from the national officers of the Machinists' union who demanded that local members end their unauthorized job action. Most of the machinists stayed out, recalling how they had been supported in their successful strike by the immigrant AT&S workers just two months earlier.

The IWW's influence with Italian workers at the east end plant was not as solid as it was with the Hungarians. Union funds were extremely limited; the defense costs for Bill Haywood's murder trial in Idaho was draining the organization's finances. But the Wobblies were not short of activists, so they sent Carlo Tresca to Bridgeport. At this point he had been in the country for less than three years. Tresca gave a speech at Sedlar Hall on July 23. The IWW now had an Italian branch in the city, but relations between that immigrant community and the Hungarian strikers continued to worsen. One morning a group of Italian workmen, presumed to be scabs, approached the picket line. Neither side could communicate with the other, and the strikers attacked them. They later discovered that the Italians were actually streetcar repairmen.

The union maintained morale by organizing family picnics with food and drink donated by neighborhood businesses. Strikers also got free haircuts and shaves, along with extended credit at local stores. National IWW figures appeared at the union's open air meetings. These events took place in the hot summer sun, with workers straining to hear the speakers who addressed them without the benefit of a sound system. Featured orators included Vincent St. John (known as "the Saint") and Elizabeth Gurley Flynn, the sixteen-year old organizer whose "fiery speeches jumped all over the large corporations," according to a newspaper report. Flynn was so effective that the authorities attempted to deny her a permit to speak. One police official complained that strike leaders "shouldn't be allowed to import young girls to speak in flowing languages causing workers to brood and go out and kill some of our prominent men."

This was Flynn's first strike and her first official organizing with the IWW. She participated in strike committee sessions, mass picketing and organizing meetings conducted in Hungarian and English. The meetings were accompanied with "sad Hungarian violin music for entertainment," Flynn recalled in her autobiography. She stayed at the home of a striking worker, sharing the single bed with a mother and her child. As part of the union's activity to build public support, the young organizer held street meetings in downtown Bridgeport. "We gained considerable support in this way, which helped to settle the strike," Flynn wrote. Before the conflict was over, Elizabeth Gurley Flynn would celebrate her 17th birthday.

By the end of the month, IWW opponents intensified their efforts. Police arrested dozens of strikers. Newspapers red-baited the strike, proclaiming that workers were under "anarchistic and socialistic" influences. The Machinists union sent in Stewart Reid, whose job was to break the solidarity of local unions with the Wobblies. The company's board of directors voted to keep the west end mills closed until August 31st, effectively locking out the strikers. The boss now publicly threatened to move his entire operation out of Bridgeport. Financial support from Hungarian businessmen began to dry up.

By August, strikers started to leave town in order to find work. Those arrested in picket line scuffles received punitive prison sentences. Machinists continued to trickle back to work under intense pressure from their leaders and the threat of losing their union membership. The company initiated a "back to work" petition among workers. The Bridgeport Central Labor Council, an alliance of local AFL unions, apparently ignored the strike altogether. On August 16th, the Council met to plan their Labor Day festivities and voted to send a donation to striking Hartford bakers. The press covered the meeting, but there was no indication that the Council members even discussed the AT&S turmoil.

The workers voted to end their strike, but only after having won a number of the changes they had demanded. The employer restored the workers' alternating day and night shifts, the issue that had first triggered the strike. Wage increases were won after an arbitration process brokered by local Hungarian businessmen, and certain foremen, despised by the strikers, were fired.

So, given a century of hindsight, how can the first IWW strike in Connecticut be evaluated? Participants and historians are divided. An essay by Robert J.

Embardo called the strike a "sugar-coated defeat for AT&S employees." The title of his article, *"Summer Lightning, 1907: The Wobblies in Bridgeport"* underscored Embardo's premise that the IWW's efforts were flashy but ineffective. He concluded that the strike's failure was a rejection of the IWW's radical ideology.

AT&S owner Frank Wilmot certainly would have agreed. The company "conceded nothing to the strikers," he boasted. The annual report of the Connecticut Bureau of Labor Statistics also recorded the strike as unsuccessful. Even the Wobblies' Vincent St. John dismissed it as a failure, writing that "the strike was lost through the scabbing tactics of the AF of L" which forced the machinists back to work.

Others called the strike a qualified success. The *Bridgeport Post*, no friend of the IWW, pointed to "minor concessions," including the re-establishment of the rotating schedule. Likewise, J.O. Johnson, a Bridgeport Wobbly, reported to the IWW's national body that the strike produced "slight concessions." The Machinist union's Stewart Reid begrudgingly wrote that "it looks like the Industrialists (IWW) will be able to claim a victory here" even though he had done his best to destroy the strike.

Those who view the labor movement as a continuum, and who understand the IWW's role in that process, give the AT&S workers their due. Labor historian Philip Foner called the strike a "significant victory,' as did the IWW's own historian Fred Thompson. Melvyn Dubofsky wrote in his IWW history *We Shall Be All* that "in Bridgeport the Wobblies welded together unskilled Hungarian immigrants and skilled native Americans in a united front which in August 1907 won important concessions." And Bridgeport labor historian Cecelia Bucki found that this early IWW effort made a lasting impact on the city's industrial and political structures for several decades, including the stunning capture of City Hall by the Socialist Party in 1933. "Far from being a repudiation of radicals," Bucki writes, "the strike actually established a strong radical presence in the Hungarian community. The subsequent history of the Socialist Party, the Socialist Labor Party, the IWW and even the postwar Communist Party in this community can be traced to the effects of this strike."

The 1907 AT&S strike was not summer lightning. Like the rest of the IWW's history, it was more like thunder, rolling across Bridgeport and reverberating throughout the twentieth century.

IWW vs. IWW

Three years after the IWW was founded, it split apart. Connecticut's Wobbly presence reflected this division, which in 1908 resulted in two "IWWs" operating in various parts of the state simultaneously.

At the IWW's first convention, where long-standing feuds were temporarily put aside, there were already cracks in the IWW's foundation. Eugene Debs wanted the new union to join the Socialist Party; the leader of the Socialist Labor Party (SLP), Daniel DeLeon, known as "the Pope" because of his air of infallibility on political matters, thought the union should go with him.

At the fractious 1908 convention, Vincent St. John was elected General Secretary, supported by Joe Ettor and others. Their headquarters remained in Chicago, along with the union's records and property. A "rump" convention was organized by DeLeon, who had been ousted by the Wobbly majority, and it held its own event in Paterson, New Jersey in November. That gathering recorded a total of twenty-one delegates, including one from Bridgeport. This group eventually moved to Detroit, and after the Pope died the "Detroit IWW" became the Workers' International Industrial Union (WIIU). The union disappeared altogether in 1925.

It should have been obvious that a single union—with twice the resources— would have greatly benefitted Connecticut's workers. And in fact, in 1906 the Hartford chapter of the SLP approached the city's Socialist Party chapter with the intention of unifying the two groups and supporting the IWW. They met, but never merged.

DeLeon did not let the recent Lawrence success interfere with his sectarian nature. He spoke in April, 1912 to a Hartford audience, just a few weeks after the Bread and Roses strike victory. He didn't mention Lawrence, but he told the crowd the SLP "did not want to tear down the laws, it advocated no anarchistical doctrines," unlike Bill Haywood's union.

When DeLeon died in 1914, there were five active IWW locals in Connecticut. Three were part of the Detroit group: Number 112, a mixed local from Bridgeport; Local 69 in Hartford composed of machinists; and the Mystic textile workers of Local 35.

The Chicago IWW had two locals: one in Moosup (303) and one in Norwalk (535), both comprised of textile workers. Despite its Willimantic victories in 1912 and the statewide IWW office set up there, the Thread City was not listed in either camp in 1914.

The WIIU attempted some organizing in Connecticut. In May of 1916, the union held an open air rally in Manchester for silk workers employed at the Cheney mills. The rally was followed up by an organizational meeting in Tinker Hall, where a local union was chartered with 75 members. The group also played a role in Bridgeport's Columbia Graphophone's series of strikes by more than one thousand workers who demanded wage increases and a 44-hour work week.

The Socialist Party of Eugene Debs—DeLeon's constant rival—had originally been supportive of the IWW's organizing. On at least some occasions, like the 1912 Willimantic campaigns, the Party had put workers together with Wobbly organizers. In later years, however, local SP leaders railed against "anarchism and sabotage" and ignored IWW strikes right in their midst.

It was the Chicago IWW, led by Haywood, Gurley Flynn, Ettor and others, which led most of the Wobbly organizing in Connecticut for the next two decades, including both their most heartbreaking defeats and their biggest victories

The Brotherhood of Machinists

"Stop right there. How many victories have you ever won?" the belligerent audience member yelled out, challenging the main speaker at a Bridgeport meeting in 1914. "I never lost a battle," Big Bill Haywood boasted.

The IWW worked hard to attract Connecticut machinists into the tent of the one big union. Joe Campbell, the Wobblies' first state organizer, was a machinist. Wobblies and machinist union members worked together closely in the November, 1906 General Electric strike in Schenectady, New York, which featured the first American sit-down strike. The same coalition played a critical role in the 1907 strike at American Tube & Stamping in Bridgeport.

By 1911, the Wobblies had established the Brotherhood of Machinists to rival the International Association of Machinists (IAM), a craft union that excluded unskilled workers even though they labored side by side in the same factories. The IAM leadership deeply resented the IWW's move onto their turf. In Bridgeport, the IWW established a Brotherhood local in the spring of 1914. Bill Haywood was invited to speak to the new union and attracted hundreds of workers to Lincoln Hall on Cannon Street. Robert M. Lackey, the secretary-treasurer of the Brotherhood, shared the stage with him, as did Joseph L. Ryan, a union musician. Haywood called the IWW a "rebel organization, a radical organization" out to challenge the idea of craft unionists who "have been dividing their house against itself."

"The American capitalists have the finest organization on the face of the earth," the Wobbly leader declared. "They have linked the mines, the railroads, the steamships, the foundries, the machine shops, the selling agencies and every other branch of industry into one magnificent machine."

"I want to tell labor men here tonight that they must do things for themselves," Haywood told the crowd. He spoke of the "new era in the history of the worker that is sweeping around the world," citing not only European struggles but Indian and Mexican workers who were uniting and organizing in their own countries. The craft strategy, on the other hand, had failed because in the metal trades alone there were 60 organizations. "There are 2,700 unions in the American Federation of Labor," Bill declared, "2,700 different working agreements all expiring at different times. What chance has one of these unions got to use its greatest weapon—the strike?"

Big Bill's speech was not without its critics. Although he urged the building of an organization that would include "every man who worked in an industry, from the floor sweeper to the pattern maker, expert mechanic and shipping clerk," he was heckled by a handful of loyal AFL members who charged that he was "preaching discord." This accusation was especially ironic considering the 1907 AT&S strikes had shown the value of solidarity between skilled and unskilled labor.

One month after Bill Haywood appeared before the Bridgeport audience, Elizabeth Gurley Flynn came to town for the same purpose. She painted a picture of the "New Unionism" for another enthusiastic crowd of machinists and other workers. Gurley Flynn was introduced by Ben Legere, who was now an IWW organizer, and John J. McCarthy, a Brotherhood general organizer from New York.

Around this same time, the IWW's Walter Eggeman was in New Haven doing a careful study of the Winchester Arms factory. His results were published in an article by Robert Lackey in the November, 1912 issue of the *International Socialist Review*, "the fighting magazine of the working class" that chronicled many Wobbly campaigns. With 6,000 workers on the payroll in a plant that covered 59 acres, Winchester was the largest manufacturer of firearms and ammunition in the world.

"Poor pay, long hours and tyrannical treatment" characterized the operation, Eggeman found. In sharp contrast, shareholders received enormous dividends and the value of the stock had risen to "$1200 for a hundred-dollar share"

according to Lackey. The company had an elaborate spy system to thwart union efforts within the plant. The boss paid workers by piece rate, even for the men whose job it was to empty the cuspidors. Despite the great wealth produced at Winchester, workers faced regular pay cuts, but never for the entire workforce. Rather, "a reduction is made in one department at a time, but every department is due for at least one cut in about every two years," Lackey wrote. Over the last decade, production had doubled but wages actually decreased.

Work in the cartridge department was particularly dangerous, Lackey reported. Seven workers had recently been killed in powder explosions, he revealed, and "the loss of a finger or an eye is not infrequent."

Winchester rivaled Colt Firearms of Hartford in the public imagination. Company-generated publicity helped craft the romantic notion of their product as "The Gun That Won the West." Of course, the weapon had its dark side. The Winchester rifle was used to break up Chicago protestors in 1886 in what became known as the "Haymarket Riot." And Winchesters were noticed by reporters in the hands of the O'Brien Agency's private detectives imported from New York to break the IWW's Blumenthal strike in Shelton.

Despite earlier unsuccessful attempts by others to organize a union, Walter Eggeman and Robert Lackey now undertook the effort. Several times a week at the shop doors or on the New Haven green they spoke to workers. The union paraded a two-sided banner in front of the plant demanding better pay, shorter hours and industrial freedom, and proclaiming the fight against the lack of overtime pay and the industrial spy system. The Wobblies distributed thousands of copies of the IWW's *Machinist Bulletin*. The local police interfered with the organizers' efforts, alleging that the handouts violated city laws. But *selling* newspapers was legal, so in response, the Wobblies distributed pennies to workers and then charged them one cent a copy.

The rival unions took turns trying to organize Winchester. The IAM mounted small strikes in 1915 and 1919 that barely made a dent in production. The IWW was back in 1916 for a brief period. It was not until 1944 that the IAM finally succeeded in organizing the rifle manufacturer. The company's ownership changed hands several times and received substantial tax breaks to maintain local jobs. Finally in 2006, Winchester left the state altogether despite a New Haven labor/community coalition that organized to keep the plant open.

The Influence of the "Bread and Roses" Strike on Connecticut

As far as Connecticut organizers were concerned, the IWW campaign with the greatest impact took place in Massachusetts, an extraordinary event that is now known as the "Bread and Roses" strike. It showed mill and factory workers everywhere that what had once been considered impossible could now be achieved.

In January, 1912, the Massachusetts legislature lowered the maximum weekly work hours for women and children from 56 to 54 hours. This change was meant to improve the lives of the state's most vulnerable workers, but the lawmakers were silent on how wages would be affected. When the hours decreased, employers also cut wages by 3 ½ per cent, about the cost of three loaves of bread.

Conditions were already desperate for families who lived in crowded and dangerous conditions. Many survived on subsistence levels; one out of two workers' children died before they reached 12 years of age.

On January 11th, Polish women working in the Everett Cotton Mills discovered the short pay and shut down their looms, urging others to join them.

Soon, 25,000 workers were on strike against the employers' wage theft and many other injustices on the job.

A small IWW local had already been active in the textile city. The Lawrence Wobblies' familiarity with the workforce aided IWW organizer Joe Ettor and Arturo Giovannitti when they came to town to lead the strike. The two men organized an effective leadership structure composed of all the many ethnic groups with meetings that were translated into 25 languages. They used new, creative strike tactics: massive, nonviolent demonstrations; "singing" mobile picket lines; the children's exodus, which sent strikers' kids to safe havens in other cities; financial support from textile workers in the region and supporters nationwide in order to fund food distribution and medical care; and special legislative hearings in Washington to investigate and publicize Lawrence conditions.

The authorities and mill owners conspired to break the strike by declaring martial law, calling out the militia, enlisting most of the religious community against the workers, and even planting dynamite to frame the IWW. Ettor and Giovannitti were falsely charged with being accomplices in the fatal shooting of striker Anna LoPizzo. They spent months in jail and their case became a worldwide cause while they awaited trial. The two organizers were eventually acquitted.

By March 12th, the mill owners agreed to most of the workers' demands, including a significant pay increase. Despite popular folklore, the "Bread and Roses" tag came about after the strike was over. The term, however, is an important signifier that still resonates. The IWW strikers demanded not only bread for sustenance but also the leisure time to enjoy life.

Wobbly organizers from Lawrence frequently stopped in Connecticut, carrying the spark of victory to Willimantic and other mill towns. The Bread and Roses strike was arguably the greatest success for the IWW. The historic event changed the lives of many of Connecticut workers.

The Children's Exodus

Preparations were complete for the massive parade through downtown Bridgeport. The children of the Bread and Roses strike were scheduled to arrive at the city's train station to a warm welcome on a cold February night in 1912. They never arrived. "There will be no more children sent from Lawrence," declared Marshal John J. Sullivan in response to the Bridgeport trip. Sullivan warned that in order to stop children from leaving his city, "I shall not hesitate to use all the power necessary." And indeed he did. The next time parents attempted to put their children on the train from Lawrence, youngsters and parents were beaten and arrested.

Some children had already been sent to New York, New Hampshire and Vermont to supportive families with the promise of good food, medical care and education. But on February 22, the Lawrence police stopped parents from putting their children on the Bridgeport train. The city was under martial law, and Sullivan declared "I will use all the resources of the law to stop these strike leaders making a show of these children on the streets to collect money for anybody or any purpose."

Organizers turned away the Bridgeport marching band and the carriages that were supposed to transport the children to a rally at Wall and Main streets. But Benjamin Legere and Matilda Rabinowitz, leaders of the local Lawrence Strike Aid Committee, already had other plans in the works to promote the strike.

Bill Haywood arrived in the city a few days later. "I'm glad to be in Bridgeport tonight," Haywood told the enthusiastic crowd at the Lyric Theatre. ""I want to rouse you, workers of Bridgeport, to the realization that the striking mill workers of Lawrence are fighting your fight." According to the *Bridgeport*

Evening Farmer, Big Bill "roused his audience to a high pitch of fervor." Only the well-known socialist leader Eugene Debs was accustomed to getting more applause, the newspaper noted.

Haywood's appearance in the city came at a time when the Socialist Party was split over its support for the IWW. The local Party chapter threatened to expel Haywood if he came to Bridgeport, foreshadowing his eventual split with the national group. "In as much as the Socialist Party is the working class, I do not quite see how I can be expelled from my class," Bill replied.

The vicious response of the Lawrence police gave the strike the national attention it needed, swaying public opinion and spurring a congressional investigation. On March 12th the Lawrence mill owners gave in and the workers had won their demands, including a 15% pay increase, no increase in hours, double pay for overtime, and a modification of the so-called bonus system. Mills throughout Connecticut and New England raised wages of an estimated 250,000 workers in order to avoid another Lawrence.

Wildfire in Thread City

When the textile workers in Lawrence, Massachusetts won their struggle in March, the victory inspired thousands of other mill workers throughout New England and paved the way for dramatic improvements in wages and working conditions.

Newspapers in Connecticut cities, especially textile towns like Willimantic, printed daily reports on the Massachusetts strike. AFL head Sam Gompers condemned Lawrence as "a class-conscious industrial revolution." John Golden of the United Textile Workers—who tried to take the strike over and when that failed, to sabotage it—labeled the Wobblies "anarchistic." Hartford's Civic League for Immigrants, which promoted the "Americanization" of European refugees, warned that communists were behind the Lawrence strike, creating a "national peril."

Just one day after the Lawrence strike ended, local officials at the Quidnick-Windham mill in Willimantic stated that it was "extremely doubtful" there would be any wage increase for their workers. Cotton prices were too high and manufacturers were "not getting enough on their finished goods to make a decent profit," a spokesman said.

But on Saturday, April 21, a dozen doffers at the Quidnick mill went on strike and demanded a raise. It was the doffers' job to take full spindles of thread off the looms, a small but vital part of the mill's operation. The company quickly agreed and their wages went from $7.25 to $7.50 a week. It was a small price to pay to keep this spark from becoming a wildfire of labor agitation.

Unfortunately for the Quidnick boss, the blaze spread anyway. By Monday, other workers learned of the doffers' victory. Seventy Quidnick ring spinners and warpers walked out. The doffers, even though they had just won their raise, walked once again in solidarity. But unlike Lawrence, the weavers had not been moved to join their co-workers.

Strikers met the next morning on Bridge Street, picketing the office of Quidnick manager W.B. Knight. Their demand was a 10% increase and the elimination of the twenty-minute period they worked each day without pay. The strikers used Lawrence as their model. Just as the IWW had staged massive "chain" picket lines, the Quidnick workers "joined hands and made a straight line across the entrance to the mills," according to a local news account. And more importantly, they knew that a victory was linked to their ability to shut down the entire company. This meant winning over the weavers.

Despite the extremely cold morning weather, the strikers approached the weavers as they walked toward the mill, urging them to join the strike. It took only a little convincing. Soon an enthusiastic crowd of 400 workers marched to the Town Hall.

The strikers agreed to send a committee to meet with the boss the next morning, and to call in a union organizer. As one worker put it, "Capital organized to look out for its interests and if it was good enough for Capital to organize it ought to be equally good for the working people." The local newspaper reported that socialists, who also spoke to the assembly, called in the IWW. The union quickly sent Benjamin Legere, the Bridgeport activist and editor.

By Thursday, the company agreed to the 10% raise the doffers and spinners' had demanded and to eliminate unpaid overtime. The weavers were denied a raise because, the company insisted, they had recently received one. But the weavers held out for 10% across the board for their department, and the doffers and spinners backed them up. The owner gave in. Industrial unity—a critical difference between the IWW and the craft unions—was a success.

Of all the mill companies in Willimantic, the Quidnick workers were the poorest. Whole families worked at the mill. They lived in sub-standard housing. Many received public assistance. Maybe because they had the least to lose, the Quidnick workers struck the first successful blow. The day after the Quidnick victory, 1,000 American Thread mill workers walked out, demanding a pay hike which they won in record time.

A week after the twelve Quidnick doffers walked out, Elizabeth Gurley Flynn was in town to address the Willimantic's mill workers. The IWW now had a foothold in the Thread City.

Bad Element in Town

At least a dozen Connecticut textile mills were affected by the IWW victory in Lawrence. In many cases Wobbly organizers played a lead role in the strikes that followed, but frequently the workers themselves, seeing what the union had achieved in the Bread and Roses strike, were inspired to act on their own.

In the weeks after Lawrence strikers won their demands, workers at the French River Textile Mill in Mechanicsville were pleased to get a 5% raise from their boss without having to walk out. But a few weeks later, 175 French River weavers were forced to run two looms each on the specialty fabric they produced, essentially doing twice the work for the same pay. They struck on April 10 and rallied at the Hibernian Hall in Putnam. Within two days they had met to plan strategy with IWW delegate Powers from Providence, Rhode Island. But as quickly as they went out, the weavers were right back to work. Immediately after the IWW meeting, the boss agreed to return them to one loom each.

Also inspired by the historic Lawrence struggle were cotton workers at the Ross Mill in Eagleville (part of Mansfield). They were in talks with their employer, who insisted he could not provide more than a 5% raise. These workers demanded 10% and staged a brief walkout. They held firm and the boss soon relented.

Other mill owners in the area did not wait for their workers to shut the mills down. The Palmer Brothers raised their New London employees' wages the day after the French River strikers had returned to work. The company announced that its Palmertown and Fitchville mill workers would soon receive the increase as well.

During this same period the largest cotton manufacturing firm in eastern Connecticut raised wages from 7 to 10% at their big mills in Grosvenordale and North Grosvenordale. The textile industry's new-found generosity came as a surprise to many. Reporting on Grosvenordale increases, one newspaper observed that "considering that a small increase was granted in 1909 when no other cotton mill raised wages, a raise this time was hardly expected."

Not every group of workers fared so well. The IWW had been working in Jewett City in May to organize 400 workers at the Aspinook Bleachery. Plants like Aspinook typically provided the bleaching, dyeing and finishing for woven cotton goods. Before a colorful print was applied to cotton fabric, it had to be pure white. Aspinook's printing department struck first, followed by another 200 workers on May 22nd. The owner enlisted the priests of St. Mary's Church who spoke out at every mass against the IWW. The union was not a labor organization at all, the priests told their parishioners, it did not believe in religion, and was a "bad element in any community." The boss refused to meet with the strikers' committee and immediately shut down the mill. The IWW's Laurie Marcotte of New Bedford organized mass meetings of the strikers in response.

Most of the strikers were Catholic and the local clergy continued to interject themselves into the union's campaign by starting a back-to-work movement. Some of the strikers resisted the priests' lobbying and on June 4th held a mass meeting on a local baseball field to hear Wobbly organizers urge them on. Soon, however, the mill reopened and a majority of workers returned.

On May 24th the French River mill workers, led by Wobblies Jean Spielman and Grover Perry, struck again. They had already defeated the two-loom scheme, but were still rankled by a system of fines that the supervisors used to take back big chunks of the raises they had won. On the strike's second day they paraded through Mechanicsville in a show of strength.

The workers demanded the reinstatement of Carrie Jasmin, a skein winder who had been fired when she challenged the boss. In addition, the workers wanted 5% raises for all classes of employees, both skilled and unskilled. They also insisted that the piece work rates be posted in the sewing department so that these workers knew what they could expect to make each week.

The mill owner announced that he would be evicting the strikers from their company-owned tenements and from the French River Inn which it also owned.

The union held a fundraising dance for strike relief and collected money throughout the town in little tin cans, reportedly the same ones that had been used during the big Lawrence strike. Donations came in from the towns of Baltic and Webster, as well as from Massachusetts and Rhode Island towns where the IWW had a presence.

The strike continued into June and the families who had been forced from their homes were leaving Mechanicsville to find work elsewhere. Solidarity remained strong, however: the daily picket line was maintained and no worker scabbed. The union even found enough money to send strikers' kids to the local circus when it came to town.

By the fourth week, strikebreakers from Philadelphia arrived. The IWW countered with its "big gun" Elizabeth Gurley Flynn, who arrived in Putnam on June 21st and pledged to reorganize the union's efforts. But three days later the local strike leader Fred Ellery was arrested after a private guard attacked him on the picket line. Despite their desperate situation, Ellery's co-workers raised

$500 to bail him out. His arrest, though, apparently broke the will of the strikers, who soon agreed to return to work with the status of new employees. Fred Ellery, who had been dubbed "the Ettor of the local strike," was brought to trial and agreed to leave town to avoid a harsh jail sentence. He asked for time to put his affairs in order, but the prosecutor insisted he pack up and get out that same day.

The Forty-Inch Yard

The boss immediately fired Carlo Amoto when he learned Amato was organizing a union at the Sanseer textile mill in Middletown. This was an attempt to "throttle the local union at its birth by discharging its leader," according to the *Bollettino Della Sera*, an Italian daily newspaper from New York. But the boss's strategy was ultimately "foiled by the brotherly loyalty of the weavers" who successfully demanded his reinstatement. Soon after the weavers' collective action saved Amoto's job, however, the boss shut the whole mill down.

That's the way the owners of Russell Manufacturing reacted to the IWW's organizing efforts in 1912. The company had seventeen mills in Middletown, Middlefield, Higganum, with the rest in Pennsylvania. They received many government orders, producing mostly webbing and belts for the military. Russell had been established in 1834, but according to the employer this was the first time workers tried to organize. E.K. Hubbard told reporters the company was proud of its "record of kindness to its help" for the past seventy-eight years.

Apparently, this "kindness" included the method used to calculate a yard of fabric. In order to be paid for producing thirty-six inches, a weaver actually had to produce *forty* inches of material. The work week was fifty-eight hours, and some departments had no lunch break. Furthermore, although the employees' morning shift began at 7:00 am, the boss insisted that work had to begin at 6:50. If you were "late," your pay was docked. The pressing room was miserably hot during the summer, but workers' complaints were ignored. Wages were 40 to 50% lower than they had been eight years earlier, even though the cost of living was now higher than ever.

Immigrant workers often lived in fear and isolation. Separated from mainstream society, they were strangers to the language and customs of New England natives. Upon arrival in the U.S., immigrant families were relegated to the worst housing and lowest paying jobs. Discrimination against many European groups, especially Italians, was a common practice by government agencies, the police department and social services. Take, for example, Paola Fazzana. She had been in the Middletown hospital earlier that year and had fallen behind in her payment for the medical care she had received. In response, local authorities had her deported back to Italy for not paying the hospital bill, a total of thirty-two dollars.

Despite this fear and lack of power, on May 23rd fifty Italian girls reported to the Russell mill, refused to work, and demanded a pay increase. Four days later, two mass meetings were held in the Middletown municipal building to organize all the Russell factories. More than 350 workers signed union cards; those who could afford it paid the IWW's one dollar initiation fee. At these meetings, the Russell workers, mostly Italian and Polish, listened to Raimondo Fazio of the Italian Propaganda League who had helped organize the Lawrence textile strike three months earlier, along with Wobbly organizer Walter Eggeman, union strike veteran Meyer Friedkin, and John Bush, a Polish worker from Willimantic who had just helped the American Thread workers. The speakers emphasized the IWW's principles. "We organize all the given workers into one big union," Eggeman told the crowd. "Then the interests of one are the interests of all, and the bosses will find that you have the upper hand. Let all the nationalities and all the crafts get together and demand their rights from the employing class."

At the meetings the workers established their demand for a nine-hour day and wage increases of up to 20% for all job categories. The workers also sent telegrams to government officials demanding the release of Joe Ettor and Arturo Giovannitti, as Willimantic Wobblies had just done. Some of the workers were hopeful that the boss would accept the union and their demands without a mass strike, but they were prepared to walk if necessary.

Eggeman and Fazio established IWW Local 203 with four branches: Italian, English, Polish and German. Carlo Amoto was elected one of the local's trustees. The morning of June 4th, a committee of workers attempted to meet with the employer. He refused, stating that the company would only meet with individual employees. The strike was on.

Acting first were the Russell facility at South Farms, the Starr mill in the Saddle Hill neighborhood, and the Rockfall mill in Middlefield. More than 400 workers walked out, and they enlisted sixty-five others to join them later that first morning. Three quarters of the strikers were women. Along with the wage and hour demands, the workers now wanted all laid-off employees from the Sanseer mill to be put back to work and that no worker be discriminated against because of union activity.

The strikers wore red cards pinned to their blouses or stuck in their hat bands. Printed on the cards were the words "I.W.W. Don't Be A Scab." Union signs were also plastered on fences, buildings and trees near the factories. The strikers passed out handbills in English and Italian, reading "It is to your common interest to obtain shorter hours and better wages, so stick together and enforce your demands."

Owner E. K. Hubbard called upstate to the Hartford police department, which promptly sent twenty officers to assist the local sheriff. Militia men on horseback rode up from New Haven. This massive armed force was needed for "moral effect," according to Hubbard, since the strikers were "so excitable." During the first days of the strike, the workers paraded to the South Farms factory in the morning, at lunch, and at quitting time. Each event was peaceful, except when Sheriff Thompson put his hand on one woman striker who was trying to dissuade a young girl from entering the mill. When he did, a dozen other strikers descended on him.

On the third day, strikers clashed with police. Scabs had come to work early and some of the strikers rushed into the mill office. A photographer was caught up in the scuffle. This was the only time that strikers' photos appeared in the newspaper. Fire hoses were set up inside the mills, ready for use against the workers. During the day, strikers gathered on Court Street and at the Municipal Building, listening to IWW speakers. Strike central was the Stella Theater which catered to the local Italian community. By quitting time, crowds of strikers showed up with whistles and bells to hoot at the departing scabs. Many women strikers brought their babies. Reports circulated that a few strikers had returned to work.

Newly-deputized students were armed with pistols and began patrolling with the local police. It was not the first time college students had been recruited to break a strike, noted IWW organizer Jean Spielman. They were "intellectual thugs," according to Ben Legere, who reported on the strike for local newspapers. When they were not breaking bones on the football field, Legere declared, they were breaking strikers' heads with baseball bats.

On June 7th more violence erupted and several Hartford cops were hurt. Some press accounts attributed the clash to a Wesleyan student deputy. When he clubbed a woman striker, other workers responded in kind, including striker Paolo DiManele, who grabbed deputies' batons. "Many neat blue uniforms were ripped during the fracas," one newspaper reported. A trolley car transporting scabs was protected by the cops, infuriating the strikers who tried to approach them. Then the fire hoses were turned on the crowd and stones were thrown at the strikers from inside the factory. The workers responded with stones and even their own shoes. Shots were fired; conflicting reports cited the wounding of one woman striker.

The boss hired trolleys on a private basis and issued free tickets to scabs. A local bakery brought in lunch. Escalating the situation once again, the state troopers showed up in full uniforms, which they normally only wore on ceremonial occasions. All were heavily armed. The militia was quartered in the company's buildings. "That the [city] is incapable of providing a sufficient number of peace officers to deal with a body of strikers...composed mostly of women is hardly believable," observed one editorial writer. In response to the brutal police actions, the Hartford chapter of the Socialist Party banned any of its members from joining "any military force that may be used against the working classes." Some delegates argued that it might be a good idea for socialists to join the militia and learn how to use firearms. The Hartford Central Labor Union also protested the violence, declaring that calling up the guard for strike duty was beneath the organization's dignity. It "lowered them to the stripe of the Pinkertons," the despised detective agency with a reputation for excessive force.

Spielman conjured up the Haymarket martyrs and the Molly Maguires to inspire the strikers, and he cautioned against violence. "We do not believe in using physical force," Spielman declared. "We possess a weapon stronger than physical force or violence; it is to use our labor power. We will quit producing."

On Sunday the strikers held a mass meeting. Wobbly organizers from Lawrence and New York addressed the crowd. A committee of strikers presented modified demands to the boss. The company again refused to budge.

Seven days into the strike, many of the workers' positions were being filled by replacements and some of the original local leaders had left town to find jobs elsewhere. The union tried hard to keep hold of the Polish workers who had joined the strike, but they were the first to return to work. Italian workers complained to the local consulate that they were being discriminated against. Reportedly, workers who did not walk out objected to the rehiring of the Italian strikers.

By June 22nd, the strike was over. But for this brief period, the immigrants of Middletown overcame their isolation and fear, standing up for dignity at work.

Are You With the Firm or the Workers?

Mill superintendent Flynn wanted to impress his boss, so he trained a friend to run *two* looms at the same time. This was unheard of in Mystic, Connecticut's velvet industry.

When the other weavers at the Rossie Velvet Company discovered the superintendent's plan, they shut down their machines and walked out. And, like other groups of mill workers in 1913 throughout the East Coast who had spontaneously stood up for themselves, they called for the IWW. Somehow they reached the "Detroit" office, even though it was Bill Haywood's Chicago group that had successfully organized in Willimantic just nine months earlier. Detroit sent organizer Rudolph Katz.

The strikers were a mixed bunch. German workers were the largest ethnic group, along with Italians and Slovaks. But considering their differences and the "privileged" position of the weavers over other jobs, the Rossie workers maintained class solidarity. Loom fixers, quillers, winders and warpers all joined the weavers in their walkout.

According to Katz, "the bosses called the loom fixers aside and asked them, 'Are you with the firm or the workers?' *'With the workers'* came the reply."

The weavers protested that running two machines at a time was impossible, especially since a velvet loom required more skill than cotton or woolen looms. Furthermore, most Rossie employees were only working part-time. Doubling a weaver's output would only increase unemployment.

By the third day of their job action—January 17, 1913—the strike was over and the workers had won. Owner Ernest Rossie agreed to drop the two-loom experiment. All the workers returned to their jobs.

One additional demand was also met, as described in Rudolph Katz's report. The superintendent's "pet" foreman was removed from the mill. He immediately left town. Local 35 of the IWW was born. By July, the weavers had won a pay increase, and the finishing room workers won a raise as well.

The Boss Gets What He Pays For

On a beautiful April morning in 1913, one hundred weavers walked to the Muller-Gloria silk mill in Norwalk. But instead of entering the plant, they paused. The workers decided that the silk looms wouldn't run that Spring day. Owner Richard Muller told a reporter that he had no idea why the weavers refused to enter the factory. He speculated that it was probably the fine weather that caused the delay. Muller was sure the employees would be back tomorrow, producing umbrella silk for which the company was well known.

A week later, the men and women weavers, mostly Polish immigrants, were still outside and had applied for a charter from the IWW. The dyers and ribbon workers were expected to join the weavers as well. The lace workers at the mill, who were already unionized, stuck with the AFL, but since silk production was halted, they soon had no work to do.

A special legislative commission in Hartford had just reported that the living wage for an individual factory worker should be at least $7 a week. But one Muller worker reported that due to the factory's piecework rate, he earned only $6.50. The weaver complained to the foreman that the paltry sum could not possibly support his family of seven. The foreman suggested to the weaver that he "just die." Then the foreman fined him 50 cents.

This and similar outrages fueled the strikers' cause. A female weaver earned $7.35 one week but found only $4.35 in her pay envelope. She complained and was told that if she didn't like it she could quit. Many workers were fined for rule infractions ranging from being late to talking on the job. Fines could be as much as $2 per incident. The penalties effectively reduced already low pay to starvation wages. As if the monetary charges weren't enough, foremen would hit workers with sticks or whips when their work failed to meet the company's standards.

The strike struggled on throughout May. Twenty workers tried to cross the picket line, but strikers scared many of them away. Women strikers camped out at an open lot near the mill, throwing stones and taunting the scabs who attempted to enter the mill. At one point a police officer demanded to know who was throwing the stones. "We all are," replied a striker, "arrest us all, I dare you!" The officer decided not to take action.

The IWW didn't have the resources to support the strikers while they were out of work, but still the strike continued. Benefit shows were organized by the union. Among the most popular were the Sunday picture shows at Lockwood Hall and the Pleasant Hour Theater. There were indications that the strikers had some political support as well. The mill owner wanted to bring in Pinkerton agents from New York and have them paid for and deputized by the City. Pinkertons were a ruthless anti-union private police force that had been effectively used against many labor strikes. The Norwalk city council refused to accept the offer, stating that the agents were not local residents. The boss hired them privately anyway.

To hear the employer tell it, the company was suffering from too much competition. Italian and German mills paid lower wages and worker quality was much higher, the Connecticut mill owner insisted. Then there was the rivalry between Muller-Gloria and Dundee Textile of New Jersey, the one other U.S. operation producing umbrella silk. And finally, public demand for a cheaper cotton umbrella was growing. Between the two companies, the umbrella business "only" brought in about one million dollars a year. "Everything we can do has been done in order to keep the cost of the production down," stated an industry representative. The underpaid silk workers surely agreed.

By June, Muller-Gloria had hired forty-five strike breakers from outside the city to get production going. Bridgeport and Norwalk constables, along with the Pinkertons, guarded the mill and the scabs' living quarters. Richard Muller even transported one constable in his own automobile. Muller was "anxious to have his help protected," he said. Now that the scabs were in the mill, Muller proclaimed that the strike had been broken.

Not everyone was ready to give up. The day after the owner's announcement, Michelina Uranowicz and Kamilia Obuchowska spotted strikebreakers boarding the trolley at Main and Broad Streets. The strikers followed the scabs and challenged them. A police constable arrested the two women but as he was taking them to the station, six male strikers approached the cop. Pinkerton agents swooped down and arrested the men. At the trial, the judge dismissed the charges for all but one striker, saying that the police didn't have enough evidence. One drunken Pinkerton was thrown out of the courtroom.

As it turned out, Muller could not keep the mill open with his strikebreakers. There were too few to do the work and they did not know the machines. The Pinkertons he had hired proved to be a burden as well. While on duty, the private detectives roughed up strikers and scabs alike, making the agency very unpopular in the city. The final straw for Muller was when a large quantity of silk was stolen while the "Pinks" were supposedly guarding the mill yard. For all the money and effort he had put into keeping out the IWW, Muller announced that he would shut down his operations indefinitely on June 17th, three months after the strike had begun.

The Riot That Wasn't

"Attempt to Organize I.W.W. Ends in Riot" read the *Hartford Courant* headline on May 19, 1913. The news described a union meeting on the previous night in Waterbury. The story suffered from two small problems: the IWW had *already* successfully organized a local in the city, and no riot actually took place.

Here's what the paper reported: "An unsuccessful attempt was made here tonight to organize a local branch of the I.W.W. at a meeting that ended in a riot. John Smeistrious of Boston made a statement which his audience took as reflecting on the church and religion, and members of the audience started outcries against him, which grew in volume until the hall was in a turmoil. The police were called and they succeeded in clearing the hall before any one was injured."

What really happened, as written by a reporter from the *Waterbury American* who was actually on the scene, differed significantly from the Hartford paper's sloppy story. Far from being an "unsuccessful" attempt to organize, the IWW had already formed a small local in Waterbury the previous fall.

One man in the audience *did* try to interrupt the speaker, who was criticizing church interference in union organizing (priests from Willimantic, Jewett City and Middletown had been outspoken in their disdain for the IWW during union drives the previous year). The heckler and his son were ejected by the meeting's organizers, and the two immediately ran to the Bank Street police station to file a complaint.

Three police officers then interrupted the Green Street meeting to look for those who had ejected the hecklers. By this time all hope for an orderly event had passed. Several more men were ejected. The police ordered the participants to go home. Meanwhile, a crowd grew outside the hall and the police decided to stick around.

Who would attend an IWW meeting to heckle the speaker? One possibility could be a disgruntled partisan of the American Federation of Labor. The Green Street building was normally rented by the AFL for $2.50 a night. In fact, the federation had a meeting scheduled there that same evening. But along came the IWW, paying out $6.00, which was the higher price set by the hall's owner for holding a "lecture." The clever move bumped the federation, and the AFL was forced to hold its meeting at a nearby church.

We Are Not Dogs

The 1913 strike by silk weavers in New London was probably initiated by the IWW. It was certainly inspired by the union's historic battle in Paterson, New Jersey that was taking place at the same time. But in the end, the city's Italian and Syrian weavers were overpowered by the employer and betrayed by the AFL's United Textile Workers union.

According to news reports, Wobbly organizers were in town shortly before a committee of the 200 weavers, both men and women, approached the head of the Brainerd & Armstrong silk mills on May 21, 1913. J.P. Taylor Armstrong dismissed the weavers' economic demands and told reporters that there would be no strike because the company had such a good relationship with its workforce.

In a written communication, the weavers' committee "respectfully requested" seven improvements at the mills, including a fifteen-percent wage increase which they said was in keeping with area wages. Many of the demands exposed a serious lack of respect from supervisors and the arbitrary policies that affected the weavers' daily work.

The B&A mills had taken on a large number of unpaid "learners" who replaced experienced weavers fired from the job, often for "a slight fault." The committee wanted learners to be paid a minimum wage of $4 a week (partly as a means to keep the easy replacement of weavers in check). In addition, when weavers were out sick, it had been the practice to place them back at their own looms when they returned. Now, for no apparent reason, returning workers were placed on looms they didn't know. And when a loom's warp broke down, a weaver might be idle (and unpaid) for days until it was repaired. The committee proposed a $6 weekly wage for weavers when the breakdown was not their fault. Finally, the committee suggested that the system of fines imposed on weavers for producing faulty goods was too severe and that "more discretion" should be used in issuing the penalties.

Armstrong's response was immediate—he rejected most of the workers' concerns. The company declared that it always treated its workforce fairly, paid the best wages, and only discharged or fined workers for cause. Armstrong did agree to a few demands, including placing returning workers back on their own looms.

The B&A company was significantly behind its competitors in at least one important aspect. In Putnam, four silk mills had just reduced hours from 58 to 55 a week without a pay cut. This fact, plus the recent news that there was a serious shortage of woolen and silk textile workers in eastern Connecticut, should have put the B&A weavers in a stronger position. One thousand mill hands were needed to fill skilled and unskilled positions, due at least in part to the migrant French Canadian workers who were staying on their farms rather than traveling to this state for the seasonal work. Greek, Syrian and Armenian help was now being recruited. Although the company insisted that its workforce was well paid, weavers' pay at Brainerd & Armstrong was below the regional average.

The weavers' committee handed the demands to the employer at 3:00pm on Wednesday, May 21st. By 4:00 pm Armstrong's rejection had been received and workers shut down the looms.

The next morning, the strikers gathered outside the Union Street entrance while the committee met with the boss. At this point, the employer's offer was to increase wages in New London to the same extent as any increase won by the IWW Paterson strikers. The committee refused the offer.

According to one newspaper report, some strikers denied any ongoing Wobbly influence in their efforts. The workers did not seem to make any attempt to organize the warping, quilling or winding departments. These areas kept working in anticipation of a short strike.

On the third day of the strike, a United Textile Workers organizer appeared. He said that union president John Golden would also soon arrive. He would continue to appear wherever the IWW was organizing textile workers in Connecticut. Golden, who was also commuting to Paterson, told the New London workers that "moderation" was the key to their success.

A local settlement worker named Jennie Fisher was assisting the strikers at the request of some of the women weavers. She acted as a translator for the Syrians and appeared with them at the mill and at the police station when needed. Apparently she provided more support for the strikers than the local Socialist Party chapter, which continued to hold its regular meetings without mention of support for the local struggle.

Most English-speaking workers could get their news about the IWW only from local newspapers that sensationalized the activities of the union. When a woman was killed in Ipswich, Massachusetts during a Wobbly demonstration, the front page stories strongly implied that the IWW organizers were responsible (two Wobblies were arrested and later released). A letter to the editor in the New London paper attacked the union as "noxious exotics from exotic climes," in other words, foreigners. Challenging the use of the strike as a weapon, the writer asked "when will they learn the lesson that capital can remain idle for an indefinite period while the laborer must either work, steal or starve?"

By Saturday, two departments fell idle because the weavers were not producing. On Monday, when eight women strikers had decided to return to work, they were dissuaded by the early presence of a large crowd in front of the mill. An elderly Syrian woman physically stopped a few potential scabs before the police arrived. The cops offered to escort the workers into the mill, but the jeers of the crowd made them change their minds. The next day, the police tried to arrest a male worker who they said was blocking the sidewalk. Several women strikers came to his aid, the situation escalated, and four strikers were arrested. They were released without bond and their cases were continued by a judge whose courtroom was filled by strikers watching the case.

On Wednesday, May 28th, the company issued an ultimatum: return to work in five days or be replaced. There were rumors that some of the few English-speaking weavers might go back. When three Syrian workers quietly visited a mill supervisor one night, seven strikers, including leaders Nicholas Deep and Kamel Moola, were arrested for assaulting them.

Over the weekend, a few employees did return to work and were forced to sleep on cots inside the mill. They were fed by a restaurant until the strikers found out where the meals were coming from and pressured the owner to stop delivery. A private detective agency was hired by B&A to protect the scabs. Only 15 of the 200 striking weavers returned by the company deadline; some were picked up at home by cars hired by the boss.

All the strikebreakers were described as "Americans" by the press to distinguish them from the immigrant Italian and Syrian strikers. When one of the most hated overseers ordered non-striking employees to operate looms, four of the Americans walked out to the picket lines. One of the workers, John Broom, said he would not help the employer break the strike. Broom spoke out against the harsh fines workers suffered, which he said were due to bad supervision by mill inspectors.

The weavers fought to maintain the strike with both persuasion and physical force. While some were arrested for threatening scabs, other strikers made appeals to Polish workers who had crossed the line. When two Poles told the strikers they were in danger of eviction, a collection was taken up for them and they rejoined the strike.

Production was down considerably, with about sixty of the two hundred looms in operation. But weavers continued to trickle back, and on June 5th John Golden held a meeting of the strikers who then voted to return to work. The company agreed to take back everyone and would accept a grievance committee of the weavers as long as they spoke English, which eliminated the most militant strike leaders. Armstrong also insisted that strikers pledge not to harass any strikebreakers, to which they agreed.

Golden's settlement was as fragile as it was meager. On June 9th, the day they returned, some strikers were provoked by a scab. A fight ensued and the company used the disturbance to lock out all the workers. The next morning enraged workers fought the police in a pitched battle. Women challenged male weavers who attempted to cross their line. They threw stones and filled bags with dust which they hurled at the cops. When one of their number was collared or hit, others attacked the arresting officer.

More police were called out and a dozen strikers were injured by police clubs. Wrote one newspaper: "The important thing is not whether the strikers are right or wrong in their industrial conflict, but whether manhandling goes in New London or not. If some of our imported friends go to the hospital or the burying ground they would only have themselves to blame."

"We are not dogs," a striker replied. "We will be as bad as they are if we cannot have some of our rights."

Armstrong used the riot as an excuse not to hire back twenty workers, including the original strike leaders. In defiance, the workers were heard to say that they wanted the IWW back. Armstrong told the papers that the company "would not be dictated to by its employees."

BRAINERD & ARMSTRONG'S
Spool Sewing Silk

They Evidently Have No Leader

The Russian and Polish workers at Randolph Clowes Company halted the production of the copper tubing and kitchen boilers that were making the company's owners very rich. Instead, more than one hundred of them stood beside their machines in the Waterbury factory, refusing to work.

The boss knew what they wanted: wage increases, overtime pay and shorter hours. He offered a modest compromise. In response, the workers went to lunch and didn't come back. Their strike had begun on this frigid cold Monday in February, 1916. "They evidently have no leader," reported the *Waterbury American*, but the IWW organizers who had been secretly meeting with the men knew better.

One night earlier, Elizabeth Gurley Flynn and her companion Anna Delish had arrived in town to address workers from a number of local factories. The police broke up the Garden Hall meeting as soon as it began, but missed the opportunity to serve an arrest warrant for Flynn when IWW organizer Louis (or Harry) Nelson distracted the authorities. Earlier that day, the cops had also failed to intercept the IWW women at the Waterbury train station.

Rumors of a strike at Randolph Clowes were everywhere on that Sunday night, but the company's president swore he knew nothing about any disturbance. "The men are contented and happy as far as I know," Charles Miller told a reporter. By Monday, Miller was offering them a raise and a shorter workweek, but the men refused the compromise as insufficient.

Strike fever had hit the Naugatuck Valley and IWW organizers seemed to be everywhere. Two hundred women at Osborne & Cheeseman textile factory struck for higher wages, and at least three other companies were on the verge of calling a strike. The Wobs were credited with the American Brass Company walk out in Ansonia where as many as 4,000 workers of nine different nationalities united and struck. Workers met in a rented hall, but when a Wobbly, possibly Joe Bonish, began to address the crowd, the hall's owner pushed him offstage and took over. The strike dragged on for more than a week as the hall owner negotiated as a "voluntary arbitrator" with the boss. His influence apparently waned and finally the workers themselves set up a well-organized picket line command without the self-appointed "leader." The Italian strikers called for the IWW's Joe Ettor to help them. American Brass first responded with a panicked plea to Hartford for state militia protection, but Governor Marcus Holcomb refused. The boss then hired a hundred goons from New York. He also returned to the bargaining table with a 15% wage hike proposal that the American Brass strikers happily accepted.

At the Randolph Clowes Company, workers were back on the job in two days. Apparently they were quite satisfied with the deal; when asked by reporters what the final settlement was, the boss refused to answer. The Wobbly organizers moved on to the next city, the next fight.

One Big Union

In a few rooms above Giolito's Restaurant on Market Street, not far from the Hartford Police Station, Sam Bernowsky hung the charter for the local branch of the Industrial Workers of the World. The document was signed by Bill Haywood, who was appealing his conviction under the Espionage Act for "conspiring to hinder the draft, encourage desertion, and intimidate others in connection with labor disputes." Sam's job was to organize Hartford's unemployed, part of the IWW's goal of organizing all working people.

It was March, 1919 and within a few weeks, hundreds of Hartford-area workers were flocking to IWW meetings chaired by Peter Kraskowsky and secretary Harry Nelson. The IWW was growing quickly among immigrant workers. Unemployment soared as soldiers were returning home from the war to reclaim their old jobs. The guarantee of a minimum wage was still being opposed by local manufacturers. Black workers were petitioning the State to end widespread discrimination. Women were organizing for the right to vote. Labor unrest was at its peak, with eighteen strikes in Hartford alone within the past year.

The official response to the union that was trying to actually organize these different communities into "One Big Union" was fast and furious. A local newspaper reported that it had discovered local IWW literature "so dangerous that complete publication is prevented." Instead, the paper printed a large photograph of the building in which the union rented with the caption "Headquarters of Reds in Hartford." Soon after the photo appeared, landlord Timothy J. Long threatened to kick the IWW out. "What good will it do to make us get out of here?' asked Harry Nelson. "We'll only get quarters somewhere else." They were soon evicted.

Similar harassment took place when the union planned a Grand Concert and Ball at the Italian Club around the corner on Central Row. The building's owner's initially rented the IWW the space, but balked at the last minute and wouldn't open up the hall on the night of the event. Young men and women, dressed for the occasion, jammed the sidewalks anyway.

Hartford Mayor James Kinsella put the police chief on alert "for when the IWW breaks the law." Kinsella was under a lot of pressure to simply round up and arrest radicals like the city of Waterbury had just done. The Waterbury raid had nabbed Sam Bernowsky who was then threatened with deportation. Kinsella, however, noted that most of those arrested in the raid had been released without charges.

Other city officials urged the state legislature to allow towns to "authorize the construction of armories within their respective limits and the issuance of machine guns to be prepared to cope with threatened uprisings." The Hartford Board of Aldermen passed a city ordinance making it a crime to carry a red flag, and the General Assembly soon followed suit. It took a group of University of Connecticut law students more than 50 years later to have that particular law overturned as an infringement on free speech. In the spirit of the times, the Hartford Fire Insurance Company began to offer strike insurance against "riots, civil commotion, and workers' occupation of factories."

Even members of Hartford's religious community got into the act. Reverend Howard V. Ross of the First Methodist Church warned upstanding native-born churchgoers about subversives and how to spot them. His public comments were directed as much at the local immigrant population as at the IWW. He told his congregation that immigrants were "a sodden, sour, bitter mass of humanity that resists the best ideals of American and Christian civilization from the lowest peasant class of Italy, with their ideas of low living and filth and poverty, to the Balkans with low instincts of society and womanhood. If you seek the anarchist, the Bolshevist, the wild-eyed turbulent radical, when you find him and look into his face, behold it is the face of a foreigner."

Not to be outdone, the Reverend Herbert Judson White laid out his plan for dealing with unemployed immigrant workers. "They ought to be treated like any other criminals," White said. "They want to live without working. Several boatloads should be deported from every state in the union."

These views did not go completely unchallenged by other church leaders. Although they would not come right out and support union organizing efforts, a number of local clergy did respond to Ross and White. Some suggested that "we should be willing to remove proven social injustice" in order to dampen the revolutionary fires that were being ignited in Hartford.

The IWW organizers picked the issue of unemployment to expose the inability of both business and government to meet the basic needs of working people. A packed rally at Hartford's Grand Theater organized by the union supported the following resolution:

> *Whereas* several thousand workmen in Hartford are willing to work but can find no employment, and

> *Whereas* if this condition continues, it will result in hunger and misery among a larger class, it is

> *Resolved* by 2,000 working people assembled in a mass meeting at the Grand Theater, that we call upon the mayor of Hartford to take immediate steps to find employment for the unemployed of this city.

The meeting was a historic event. The house was standing room only, jammed with workers dressed in their Sunday clothes. They cheered the speakers who delivered their talks in Polish, Russian, and English. They responded enthusiastically to verbal jabs at the inflammatory news coverage targeting the IWW. As one organizer exclaimed, "we aren't going to have any violence, even if the editor of the *Hartford Courant* wants it!"

Mayor Kinsella's response to the crowd's demand for employment was to announce that 300 jobs were available at the Trout Brook Ice Company in New Hartford. The actual number of job openings, as well as the safety of working conditions at the plant, was disputed by others. City and state employment figures showed that there were thousands of workers who could not find jobs.

One speaker at the Grand Theater put the question succinctly. Michael Rosenberg, a veteran of the recent "great war" himself, spoke for more than just Hartford's unemployed when it was his turn to address the crowd: "We say to President Wilson and to Congress: while this war was on, you appropriated billions for the war. How much are you willing to appropriate for peace and for jobs?"

Black Workers and the IWW

Clifford Davenport begged the assembled business leaders to cooperate. If black workers weren't able to find jobs in Hartford, he said, they would join the Bolsheviks!

In 1919 Davenport was a local official with the U.S. Employment Service, and he was concerned about the "practically universal prejudice" against African American and foreign-born workers by Hartford employers. These workers couldn't find jobs, even though they were returning as World War I veterans with practical skills and experience. They were "fairly good citizens" now, he pleaded, so don't increase their discontent by denying them work. Maybe they could be scattered about in different departments to avoid a concentration of too many negroes in any one place, Davenport suggested.

In its first three decades of existence, the IWW was the only union that consistently welcomed African American workers into its ranks, fighting for their right to dignity and decent employment. At the founding convention, Bill Haywood made special note of the AFL affiliates that officially excluded black workers.

The Wobblies practiced what they preached. African American IWW organizer Ben Fletcher was instrumental in one of the union's most successful organizing drives among Philadelphia dockworkers. In 1917 he was arrested in a government round-up for "conspiring to strike" and was sent with other Wobs to Leavenworth prison. Building racial solidarity within the working class provided just one more reason for business and government to target the union for destruction.

The November, 1919 coordinated raids ordered by U.S. Attorney General A. Mitchell Palmer smashed labor networks in Connecticut by rounding up radicals and union activists on vague charges and unfounded accusations of sedition. Just days before the mass arrests, the New London Day publicized the federal government's "report on the subject of radicalism and sedition" in a story entitled "Radicals Trying Hard to Cause Revolt Among Negroes."

The report was written by a "trained investigator from the Department of Justice" and warned against a "certain class of negro leaders" who were determined to oppose the government and "the established rule of law and order." The report focused on "the identification of the negro with such radical organizations as the I.W.W.," along with the dangers posed by African American outrage about the current epidemic of lynchings in the South. The article quoted one black writer who argued support for radical groups: "Just as by joining the

I.W.W. in large numbers we forced the A.F. of L. to open its doors to us, so by joining the Socialist Party we can force belated justice and consideration from the Republicans."

The Justice Department quoted another editorial from a black journal which stated: "The negro must engage in direct action. He is forced to do this by the government. When the whites speak of direct action, they are told to use their political power. But with the negro, it is different. He has no political power. Three-fourths of the negroes of the United States are disenfranchised. It is simply logical for him to throw his lot with the Industrial Workers of the World." In part because the first great migration of black workers from the rural South had not yet reached its peak in Connecticut, the IWW found almost all its success with white immigrant workers.

Missing from the government's bigoted analysis of African Americans was the fact that black families lived in dire poverty, were excluded from good jobs, forced into substandard housing, provided inferior education, and lived in fear of racist attacks.

In 1908, a special committee in Hartford documented discrimination against black families in housing. The reaction to conditions would leave a viewer "discouraged and broken-hearted," according to the report, citing dangerous and crowded conditions and poor sanitation. The committee quoted the tenement house commission of New York City, which wrote that Hartford had "the worst housing conditions in the country" for a city its size.

Ten years later, Hartford's Board of Health reported that the infant mortality rate for black children was *178 per one thousand*, as compared to 20 per 1000 for the rest of the city's population.

Local African Americans couldn't have turned to the traditional labor unions at this time even if they wanted to. "We are united to fight for a man's place in the field of industry, and to help broad-minded people make all jobs safe for democracy, in spite of the undemocratic labor unions," declared Reverend W.B. Reed, pastor of Hartford's Shiloh Baptist Church and president of the Colored Men's Civic League in 1918.

The creation of the Congress of Industrial Organizations (CIO) in 1938 carried on the IWW's challenge to the AFL's "benign racism" of the craft unions. The AFL's closed-door policy in Connecticut, particularly in the building trades, was successfully challenged by black workers in the 1950s.

Wouldn't It Be Better to Split a Little More Kindling Wood?

Reaction & Repression

Whenever a new species of plague breaks out we desire to know at once what it is and how it can be cured. So it is with the industrial plague.
— George Pope

The IWW is the most bitterly attacked and most deliberately misrepresented of all labor organizations today.
— National Civil Liberties Bureau (1914)

REACTION & REPRESSION

In the period between 1918 and 1920, the IWW was the target of a massive assault by the federal government from which it never fully recovered. The attack was aided by industry, the AFL, political parties, religious leaders, and most of the nation's newspapers. All of these groups felt threatened by what the Wobblies were attempting to accomplish: one big union that could tip the scales of power away from the establishment to the vast majority of the population—the working class.

But jailing Wobbly organizers, framing their leaders, smashing their offices and killing their activists could not completely eradicate the IWW. Even its own errors and internal conflicts did not extinguish the Wobbly flame. Throughout the 1920's and beyond, the union continued to organize in the fields and forests, on board ships and on the docks, and on farms and factories. The Wobblies even established union branches across the globe as far away as South Africa and Australia.

The legacy of the IWW continues today despite all the attempts to erase it. The CIO, for instance, benefited from the experience of many former IWW organizers. Labor radical and CIO activist Len DeCaux wrote that "when the CIO lefts let down their hair, it seemed that only the youngest had no background of Wobbly associations."

Today the IWW is much smaller but just as feisty. It has become a pioneer in nontraditional or alternative union organizing. Along with many other efforts by groups that are not always affiliated with traditional unions, present-day Wobblies seek to unite marginalized workers from bike messengers to bakers.

Despite the repression it has faced, the IWW's vision still shines through. As Joe Ettor, fighting for his life in a Lawrence courtroom, told the judge and jury: "If an idea can live, it lives because history adjudges it right...the scaffold has never yet and never will destroy an idea or movement."

No Anarchists on Board

The SS Caronia sailed from Liverpool in October 1910, picking up passengers on its way to New York. Two sisters traveling to Hartford, Catherine and Ella Abrams, got on at the port city of Queenstown (now Cobh) in County Cork, Ireland. There were more than 1300 passengers aboard, but no anarchists.

Catherine and Ella had to answer twenty-nine questions before they could travel. Question number 21 was: Are you an anarchist? The young women answered no, and naturally every other passenger did as well.

Since 1819 Congress had required ships' captains to provide manifest lists for all their passengers. In 1910, the Immigration Act was amended to exclude criminals, paupers, and diseased persons. The Abrams had to swear they were not polygamists or "deformed or crippled." And they had to make it clear that they were not affiliated in any way with the likes of the Haymarket martyrs or Leon Czolgosz, the assassin of President William McKinley in 1901.

More than one thousand non-citizens were passengers on the Caronia trip. Most were laborers, farm hands, or servants. They were on their way to join relatives in the new world for the prospect of a better life. Catherine and Ella were going to meet their married sister Margaret Cannon who lived at 183 Lawrence Street in Hartford.

A first-class traveler like author Somerset Maugham (who wrote *Of Human Bondage*) did not face the same scrutiny, even though he was aboard the Caronia on the same voyage as the Abrams. Katherine Carroll of Limerick was not so lucky. Her records note that she was detained for further investigation.

Catherine Abrams became a housemaid for a well-to-do Hartford family; Ella was hired to work as an operator at the non-union Pope automobile factory. Colonel Pope's managers kept a close eye on Catherine and her co-workers. The company did not want a repeat of a successful union campaign that had taken place at its Toledo, Ohio factory.

The laws created to restrict immigration were in place. Along with the updated federal Espionage and Sedition Acts, they would be used against the Wobblies and other activists in the Red Scare.

Damage Control

Of all the lies told about the IWW, none was more effective than the one about sabotage. In fact, Wobblies used sabotage all the time on the job, but its definition was so twisted by employers and the press that the word came only to mean bloody violence, and Wobblies did not rely on violence against property or people—even scabs—to win their fights.

In reality, the Wobs taught that sabotage was a form of *organized inefficiency* by workers. It was a "short day's work for a short day's pay." It was working to rule, which means following all the employer's policies to the letter, a practice that inevitably ends up in workplace chaos. And as Arturo Giovannitti told an audience in New Haven, sabotage can mean exposing unsanitary practices by spotlighting unhealthy working conditions, thereby causing the public to shun an employer's product, particularly in the food industry.

Unfortunately for the union, sabotage was the wedge issue for many on the left. Many socialists distanced themselves from the IWW's militancy by proclaiming that they did not favor the tactic.

At the turn of the century there were no public relations firms that unions could hire to help them spin their image, and even if there were, the IWW would not be using them. So they got their message out through their newspapers, songs, soapbox orations and speaking tours.

Elizabeth Gurley Flynn was one of the most successful speakers the IWW ever had. She embarked on a tour that rolled into Hartford in January, 1914. At Columbia Hall, she kicked off an IWW organizing drive and explained what the union meant by sabotage. For more than ninety minutes the 23 year-old organizer mesmerized the large crowd:

"Nothing has been more misrepresented than sabotage. I am here to take the bull by the horns and explain what it means. Workingmen have exhausted every peaceful means of improving labor conditions. They have begged for improved conditions but labor gets no sympathy when it pleads with the employer. The employer is a hard headed businessman who keeps his heart in a water tight compartment.

"But when a committee went to him and told him that all the employees had decided on a price list just as the manufacturers got together and made up a price list and when he was informed that the employees demanded this price list he gave serious consideration to the matter. In this way the workers had been able to accomplish what tears had never accomplished for them.

"The struggle between capital and labor is determined by power. If the employer had the power to starve the employees back to work he won. If the employees had the power to cripple the business, they won. The strike is open warfare while sabotage is the guerrilla warfare carried on day to day.

"I am not in Hartford to justify sabotage on moral grounds. Morality is one phase of human thought. If one is to talk of morality of sabotage he might as well talk of morality of child labor, prostitution, etc. He might as well talk of the morality of working girls in the department stores for $2.50 a week and making them fit subjects for the street. When one talks of these things it is found that morality is all on the side of labor.

"Sabotage originated from the peasants of France, 'sabots' being wooden shoes. The entire word means to go clumsily like a person wearing wooden shoes. Sabotage means the withdrawal of efficiency by an efficient worker, it means for a worker to limit production to his wage. It is not a new creation of the IWW what every intelligent worker does instinctively. Sabotage is limiting one's day work to a value of $1.25 because the wage paid is $1.25. The IWW feels that an unfair day's work for an unfair day's pay is as logical as a fair day's work for a fair day's wage. Work on that basis is no crime unless laziness, which it might be called, could be regarded as a crime.

"Frederick Sumner Boyd was arrested and convicted during the Paterson strike on the charge of advocating the destruction of property. He did not advocate any such thing but said he had urged the practice of sabotage. He told the workers to use a chemical in the dye but the newspapers had not explained that this chemical was already in use [by the employer to produce a greater volume of adulterated "silk" fabric]. Boyd had simply advocated the sufficient use of the chemical to expose the fraud. I call this "open mouthed" sabotage, where workers expose the truth about articles they manufacture.

"When sabotage becomes a crime, wage slavery is legalized. Sabotage is one weapon the worker has and he needs it right here in Hartford to fight the conditions in the factories. And you know how rotten those conditions are: ten hours a day, low wages, slack seasons."

Two years after her Hartford appearance, Flynn wrote a pamphlet entitled *Sabotage* that was published in October, 1916 by the IWW and sold for ten cents. The union pulled it from their official literature list a year later when public pressure became too great. Shortly after the 1919 Palmer Raids devastated the union in Connecticut, the IWW's General Executive Board approved a resolution that stated the union "never has believed in or advocated either destruction or violence as a means of accomplishing industrial reform." Despite all its public pronouncements, the union couldn't win the PR battle over sabotage.

While the topic of her talk was controversial, Flynn's trip to Hartford was a success. She signed up new members that night at Columbia Hall, creating the first IWW chapter in the city.

The High Cost of Organizing

Salvatore Schillaci and young Angelo Del Grosso teamed up in 1917 to recruit for the IWW in Bristol, a small city of clock makers and doorbell manufacturers. Schillaci found brief employment at the Bristol Brass and New Departure factories but quit when the results of his agitation did not produce quick results. He left briefly for Ansonia but returned to work in Bristol as a carpenter at the G.J. Lacourse Company and then as a day laborer.

Finally, he and Del Grosso put together enough money to hire Empire Hall on April 17 and print flyers announcing the formation of an IWW branch in the city. Both men had been watched since their recruiting efforts had begun; now the police took action. Schillaci was arrested the day before the big meeting and was held overnight. He was charged the next day with breach of the peace and vagrancy, but the only evidence produced by the prosecutor was his Wobbly membership and some literature found in his room. Del Grosso was also arrested and held by the police.

Schillaci offered to leave town but the judge had other ideas: his case was continued and he was held on $500 bail. The money was quickly raised, so the judge increased the bail to $5,000. In addition, the State Police were called in to see if they could prove that Schillaci was an "alien anarchist" and thus eligible to be deported to Italy. The Wobblies were moved to the Hartford jail.

On May 2nd they were in court again. Angelo Del Grosso, who was eighteen years old, was found guilty of breach of the peace and ordered to serve a six-month jail sentence. Schillaci, still unable to make bail, was sent to Boston and held by the U.S. Department of Justice while their investigation continued. This gave the local press time to stir up a case against him. IWW song lyrics were published in the local paper as evidence that he was a member of the "alien enemy class"; both songs were parodies of well-known hymns and folk tunes, but apparently the newspaper had no sense of humor. One song "exalts the tramp, the hobo, the inexcusable parasite on the public," complained a local editorial.

"The State should see to it at once that every tramp is interned in a labor camp." A letter to the press called the IWW "blasphemous, degenerate and fanatical."

Apparently, Bristol handled its troublemakers more severely than surrounding towns. In Middletown, a young man had recently been fined $25 and put on probation for insulting President Wilson and the American flag. But in Bristol when a man refused to stand for the "Star Spangled Banner," two Spanish American war veterans manhandled him. He was arrested and sentenced to three months jail time by the same judge who had presided over Schilacci's case.

Finally, one month after he had been arrested, Salvatore Schillaci was returned to Bristol. The government could not find cause for his deportation. Instead, he was sent to jail for sixty days for breach of the peace.

Young Seeds of Sedition

Fifty young men, all dressed in blue uniforms, performed their military drill for appreciative onlookers. Mary Hall was proud. She was sure this was the way to keep Hartford kids from becoming Wobblies.

Miss Hall was in charge of the Good Will Cadets, an organization that worked to "squelch the demon of unrest that pervades even the consciousness of the exceedingly younger generation," through games, competitions and academics at the Good Will Club. In all, 150 young people graduated on March 20, 1919.

Too many youngsters haunted IWW and Bolshevik meetings, Mary Hall warned. If these young social radicals tried to infiltrate the cadets, "she shoves them into the street," one newspaper reported. There would be no talk of "class struggle, proletariat, or the wage system" at the Good Will Club. It was alarming to Hall that children as young as eight years of age were engaged in "wreaking vengeance on young reactionaries." She blamed parents, who gave their kids these ideas at home or took them to labor meetings. Mary Hall was determined to stamp out the seeds of sedition.

A New Species of Plague

Colonel Burpee told the banquet crowd that it was the duty of his Home Guard to appear on Connecticut streets regularly in order to "restrain sedition." He was, of course, talking about the IWW. The dinner, held in 1918, ended with bugle calls, military music, and a magic act. The guests, military officials and businessmen, were celebrating the first anniversary of the Connecticut Home Guard, forerunner of the National Guard. They met at the State Armory on Capitol Avenue in Hartford, the fortress specially created and built to defend against homegrown unrest.

Throughout the decade there was a steady call from Connecticut politicians, clergy, and newspapers to put down the IWW by any means necessary. The *Norwich Bulletin* had called for the wholesale deportation of Wobblies as early as 1912. In addition to anti-union bias, these protests frequently smacked of racist anti-immigrant sentiment.

Hartford businessman Clarence Whitney did more than just talk about the IWW. He contributed $50,000 to stop Wobbly influence in factories around the state. He provided no details on how the money would be used, but an industry of anti-labor spies and gun thugs had developed wherever the IWW organized. It is not hard to believe that some of Whitney's funds found their way to "extra-legal" activities designed to harass and assault union organizers.

Old George Pope got into the act. The Hartford industrialist, who had produced Pope automobiles and bicycles on Park Street, was now the president of the National Association of Manufacturers. He used his bully pulpit to target the IWW. "Treat the Industrial Workers of the World as we would any other band of brazen traitors!" he told the *New York Sun*. "Whenever a new species of plague breaks out we desire to know at once what it is and how it can be cured. So it is with the industrial plague," Pope declared.

Often, the IWW "threat" was fabricated by the press and other willing accomplices. When the Rev. Paul Rocchini of New Britain received a letter from two local Italian workers, it was called a "threat by anarchists." Actually, the letter was signed by D. Viola and V. Segata and was issued as a challenge to Rocchini's unfounded accusation that local donations to the Lawrence strikers had been misappropriated. In Rockville, Reverend Percy Thomas used his Memorial Day sermon to criticize the "No God, No Master" slogan raised by anarchists that had appeared at an IWW rally.

Former President William H. Taft took time from retirement in 1914 to address religious educators in New Haven, criticizing the "hysteria and misguided enthusiasm" of men like Bill Haywood. Another former politician, Carl Minkley, also chose New Haven around that time to castigate Haywood, calling him a windbag who was an anarchist but too afraid to admit it. Minkley had been a Socialist member of the Wisconsin legislature.

The Socialist Party in Connecticut had established a rightward course by its 1912 state convention. The event, which took place on Asylum Street in Hartford, nominated Samuel Beardsley for Governor. Charles Peach of Waterbury told the delegates that "trades unionism was not strong in Connecticut," ignoring the recent stunning IWW victories in Willimantic textile mills. He lamented that union organizing was not a "predominant idea with socialists." Peach received applause when he condemned sabotage and the "extreme methods for which anarchists call."

Opposition to the IWW came from organized labor too. The AFL was competing with the Wobblies for members, usually as long as they were craft workers who could easily be recruited, preferably without a strike. Ira Orburn, head of the Connecticut Federation of Labor (CFL), warned that the money collected by the IWW and "Bolsheviks" for imprisoned Tom Mooney was really being diverted for nefarious purposes. Mooney was a labor leader

UNLOADING BRIDGEPORT REDS IN HARTFORD

Police and government agents "assisting" in the loading of the 45 Bridgeport Reds on the police patrol yesterday afternoon at the Union Station.

convicted by perjured testimony of setting off a bomb at a Preparedness Day parade in San Francisco.

Ira Orburn's criticism of the IWW did not impress business leader Clarence Whitney. When the industrialist donated his $50,000 to disrupt the Wobblies, he earmarked some of the money to interfere with Orburn's CFL as well.

Hartford labor union officials tried to use the threat of the IWW boogeyman as leverage with local manufacturers. "Some are apprehensive the IWW is going to come," a Central Labor Union resolution of 1913 read. Hartford Federation president William Partridge told employers "we believe in arbitration and conciliation... against the principles of syndicalism and sabotage."

After the fierce battles in Lawrence and Paterson, Middletown, Bridgeport and Willimantic, the drumbeat against the IWW grew increasingly louder. Then came 1919.

The Red Menace

It was November 1919, and in Hartford the "Red Scare" against the IWW was heating up. The local Post Office confiscated, and the FBI was investigating, hundreds of mysterious postcards addressed in red ink and bearing only a large question mark engulfed in flames. According to authorities, the cards were thought to be warnings to Hartford radicals. In surrounding towns, fire departments pledged themselves to "fight reds," and the state prison warden brandished a revolver, declaring that he too was ready for the Red Menace. A Sunday sermon at the Asylum Hill Congregational Church denounced the anarchy of labor disturbances sweeping the country. Not to be outdone, a local newspaper ran an editorial cartoon, which showed Uncle Sam throwing an anarchist off a cliff, over the caption "Treat 'em Rough!"

For progressives, 1919 was a dangerous year: those who backed national health insurance were labeled "parlour-radicals." Two Hartford High Debating Club members were harassed and almost expelled for suggesting that industrialists, not socialists, were more harmful to the country and should be deported. Most ominously, plans were being made for a permanent detention camp for activists whose "actions or utterances" were not in the best interest of U.S. security. In May, almost 200 workers had already been arrested at the IWW's Bank Street headquarters in Waterbury, all for trumped-up charges.

For Mark Kulish, November was particularly dangerous. Kulish, a worker at Colt Firearms factory, was one of 100 Connecticut men rounded up beginning on November 7th — "Bloody Friday." They were imprisoned in the Seyms Street jail on suspicion of being subversives. For almost two months they suffered harsh conditions without trial and often without the benefit of legal counsel.

Conditions for those imprisoned amounted to torture. *The Nation* protested "the suffocation nearly to death of Peter Musek, Alan Dimitroff and Semeon Nakwhat in the 'steam room' of the Hartford jail." The charge was based on an independent investigation by legal experts into the treatment of thousands of prisoners. The published report was highly critical of the government's handling of the prisoners' detention, forcing Palmer to defend himself at a congressional hearing.

The Connecticut round-up was practice for the 1920 nationwide dragnet spearheaded by United States Attorney General A. Mitchell Palmer. Palmer's raids were designed to stem the IWW's successful organizing as well as to stamp out the inspiration workers found in the 1917 Russian revolution.

Mark Kulish's "crimes" were typical of the circumstantial charges leveled against the radicals. Area civic leaders dismissed the accusations against him and other Russian-born workers as "hysteria." Kulish and fifty-two of the Hartford detainees, mostly Wobblies and other activists, were sent to Ellis Island in New York to join hundreds more, including famous anarchist Emma Goldman, to await deportation to Russia.

The local raids fueled the hysteria of the times in sometimes absurd and tragic ways. As it turned out, the mysterious "question mark" postcards were actually a promotional gimmick to publicize a Catholic anti-Bolshevik movie entitled "The Burning Question." And Mark Kulish? A few days after his trip to Ellis Island, it was reported that the gun parts and blueprints in his possession were materials for a machine class he taught for immigrant workers.

Six months after the Hartford arrests, local officials and the national Department of Immigration were criticized by Washington's Louis F. Post, Assistant Secretary of Labor. While careful not to ascribe blame to individuals who handled the cases, Post's admonition clearly pointed out the abuses suffered by those who were jailed. He charged that in many cases, bail had been set higher than listed on the warrants, prisoners were held incommunicado, immigrant workers were not advised of their right to legal representation, and those with lawyers were refused access to them. Family members and friends were arrested when they visited the jails. Post also found that no interpreters were provided for non-English speaking prisoners. In addition, he charged that bail was not returned to those who had been able to afford it, and that local officials failed to show that those who had been arrested were truly dangers to national security.

The Palmer Raids accomplished what they set out to do: they struck at friendships and families and curbed the struggles for decent working conditions and progressive social change that had been championed by the Wobblies.

Connecticut Red Laws

Employers and politicians used brute force to stop the Wobblies. But they also had other tools at their disposal. Local and state governments were uniformly hostile to IWW organizing and usually to all labor union efforts. Here are some of the laws designed to legalize repression of the IWW and other radicals that were passed at the urging of the state's industrial powers.

An Act Concerning Seditious Utterances
Be it enacted by the Senate and House of Representatives in General Assembly convened:

Section 1. No person shall, in public or before any assemblage of ten or more persons, advocate in any language any measure, doctrine, proposal or propaganda intended to injuriously affect the government of the United States or the state of Connecticut.

Section 2. Any person violating any of the provisions of this act shall be fined not more than one thousand dollars or imprisoned not more than three years or both. — *Approved, May 2, 1913*

An Act Concerning the Improper Use of Red Flags
Be it enacted by the Senate and House of Representatives in General Assembly convened:

Section 1. Any person who shall carry or display a red flag or any other emblem as a symbol calculated to, or which may, incite people to disorder or breaches of law, shall be fined not more than two hundred dollars or imprisoned not more than six months or both. — *Approved, March 19, 1919*

Hartford Red Flag Law
Be It Ordained by the Court of Common Council of the City of Hartford:

Section 1. It shall be unlawful for persons to assemble for the purpose of advocating the overthrow of the government of the city, the state, or of the United States; and it shall be unlawful for person or persons to display in any parade, assembly, or other meeting place, the "Red Flag" or any insignia of any organization or group of persons who advocate the overthrow of any of said governments; and it shall be further unlawful for any person or persons to give, sell, or in any way distribute literature, or other propaganda published in the interests of or spreading the doctrines of such organizations or groups of persons.

Section 2. Persons so meeting or assembling, or displaying such "Red Flag" or other unlawful insignia as herein-before provided, or persons so spreading such literature or other propaganda may be arrested and forthwith brought before the police court, or if it not be in session, may be confined in the station house in said city, until the next day upon which it shall be holden, and every such person shall be punished by a fine not exceeding $100 or by imprisonment not exceeding six months or both. — *Approved March 24, 1919, Hartford Board of Aldermen*

From An Act Concerning the Misuse of the Flag

Be it enacted by the Senate and House of Representatives in General Assembly convened:

Section 1. Any person who...causes to place any inscription...upon any flag...of the United States or state flag...or who publicly misuses, mutilates, tramples upon or otherwise defaces or defiles any of said flags...shall be fined not more than one hundred dollars or imprisoned not more than six months or both, for each offense. — *Approved May 1, 1919*

An Act Concerning Sedition

Be it enacted by the Senate and House of Representatives in General Assembly convened:

Any person who shall speak, or write, print and publicly exhibit or distribute, or who shall publicly exhibit, post up or advertise any disloyal, scurrilous or abusive manner, concerning the form of government of the United States, its military forces, flag or uniforms, or any manner which is intended to bring them into contempt or which creates or fosters opposition to organized government, shall be fined not more than five hundred dollars or imprisoned not more than five years or both. — *Approved, May 13, 1919.*

From An Act Concerning the Militia

Be it enacted by the Senate and House of Representatives in General Assembly convened:

Section 7. ... If any person or persons resisting the laws of the state or unlawfully or riotously assembled, shall be injured or killed by any of the organized militia or national guard called for service in such cases, every member of the organized militia of national guard so called out shall be discharged from all civil or criminal liability therefor. All active members of the organized militia or national guard shall, except for treason, felony and breach of the peace, be privileged from arrest and imprisonment by civil authority while under orders in the active service of the state, from the day of the issuing of such orders to the time when such service shall cease. — *Approved, 1919*

GUARDING APPROACH TO MILLS, LAWRENCE, MASS. 1/12

Heroes & Martyrs

> It's not the rebels that make the troubles;
> it's the troubles that make the rebels.
> — *Irish traditional*

> There is no organization in existence having less room for hero
> worship than the Industrial Workers of the World.
> — *Paul Brissenden*

HEROES & MARTYRS

The IWW produced strong, colorful and even visionary leaders who captured the imagination of working people in Connecticut and across the country. The quote on the previous page from Paul Brissenden, a contemporary who chronicled the IWW from its birth, refers to the Wobblies' desire to achieve a collective leadership throughout its rank and file membership.

If the stories in this book show anything, it is that none of the high-profile Wobs could have succeeded without the heroic actions of the men, women and children who faced scorn and deprivation, private armies and state militias. They chose the IWW of their own free will, and by making that choice, provided courageous examples of the true definition of heroism.

The IWW was unique in that "it made no fetish of leadership, it developed no bureaucratic pyramids," according to labor historian and activist Staughton Lynd.

Eugene Debs was one of the IWW's founders. But even he warned against hero worship: "I wouldn't want to lead you out of the wilderness," Debs once said, "because if I led you out, someone else could lead you right back in."

The Undesirable Citizen Comes to Hartford

The summer light was fading and the new electric lights crackled with energy as they lit up Germania Hall. The enthusiasm of the crowd inside grew on this June night in 1908. When William D. Haywood finally stepped onto the stage, he was greeted with an explosion of applause and cheers. The labor leader was stumping for the presidential candidacy of Eugene Victor Debs, but the excited Hartford crowd had come to see "Big Bill."

Haywood, then secretary-treasurer of the Western Federation of Miners, had been labeled an "undesirable citizen" by no less than President Theodore Roosevelt. Bill and two other union officials had been on trial in 1907 for conspiracy to murder the former Idaho governor Frank Steunenberg. During the trial, union activists packed Hartford's Parsons' Theater to hear the latest news and pass a resolution demanding that the three men be released.

The Haywood trial had been a national sensation. Each day, dispatches were sent to newspapers around the country, covering every detail of the story. Why did the real murderer, Harry Orchard, implicate Haywood? Why did another witness confess and then recant? Could Bill get a fair trial? Newspapers like the *Bridgeport Post* printed daily front page photos and artist sketches of the union leader, his wife and daughter, defense attorney Clarence Darrow and prosecution witness James McParlan, the notorious Pinkerton detective who manufactured evidence against the unionists and had been responsible for the 1877 convictions of a group of rebellious Pennsylvanian miners known as the Molly Maguires. The "not guilty" verdict was finally delivered on a July morning in the Boise courtroom, but that didn't stop the government from continuing to target Haywood and other Wobbly leaders.

The trial presented such a gripping real-life drama that it was turned into a New York stage play. The Kalich Theater, located in the Bowery district, played nightly to crowds who watched the reenactment of the Boise case. On June 10, 1908 a large man appeared on stage at the end of the play and condemned Secretary of War (and presidential candidate) William Howard Taft. The "actor" was actually Bill Haywood himself. According to one news account he made a "truly dramatic appearance" before two thousand appreciative theater goers.

A week after his Broadway debut, Haywood traveled to Hartford to speak on behalf of Debs, who had been nominated in Chicago for president by the Socialist Party a month earlier. The crowd expected more than just a stump speech, and Bill didn't disappoint. His talk was entitled "Socialism and Unionism," two

STUDY OF HAYWOOD IN COURT

THIS STRIKING SKETCH OF SECRETARY W. D. HAYWOOD, WHO IS ON TRIAL AT BOISE, IDAHO, CHARGED WITH THE ASSASINATION OF FORMER GOV. STEUNENBERG, WAS DRAWN IN THE COURT ROOM ON THE FIRST DAY OF THE TRIAL.

controversial topics at a time when the government was cracking down on such dangerous ideas. In April, President Roosevelt had armed federal authorities with brand new weapons to protect the public against people like Haywood and Debs. The Attorney General had just ruled that the president could arrest radicals by using his power to prohibit the use of U.S. mail "for the advocacy of murder, arson and treason." Roosevelt told Congress that even more laws were needed to curb anarchy. "When compared with the suppression of anarchy, every other question sinks into insignificance," Roosevelt warned the lawmakers.

Teddy wasn't the only one with anarchism on the brain. A national conference of U.S. assistant district attorneys was figuring out how to stop the influx of immigrants who had "anarchistic tendencies." Every activist was suspect. Alexander Berkman had just been released from a New York court for a bomb explosion that had taken place during a Union Square rally. Locally, James Barry and James Murphy were in jail simply for distributing handbills to workers at the Torrington Hardware Company. The two were branded as agitators and held on a bail so high they couldn't post it.

This political fear of the "other" had its roots back in 1798 with the federal Alien and Sedition Acts, designed to thwart those who opposed the new American government.

Sharing the Hartford stage with Haywood was Luella Twining, one of about a dozen women who had attended the IWW's Chicago founding convention in 1905. She was a voting delegate at that historic meeting and chaired the ratification session. Now she was in charge of Haywood's east coast tour for the Socialist Party.

Luella urged listeners to vote for Debs. "He is the only candidate who is pledged to assist the army of the unemployed," she told the crowd. Joblessness was a nationwide problem, and in Hartford's north end, twenty-one tramps had recently been slapped with harsh jail sentences for sleeping in a barn on Fishfry Street. IWW representative Samuel Stodell had told a New York convention that there were almost five million unemployed workers in the United States.

Haywood spoke to the Hartford crowd about the history of Western Federation of Miners, of which he was a founder. Although the IWW was already three years old, press accounts didn't mention the leading role he played in the One Big Union's birth.

Big Bill went on to describe socialism in distinctly syndicalist terms, where workers would run society through their unions. According to Bill, a Congress of workers would represent each branch of industry, state governments would be abolished, and the means of production and distribution would be controlled by the working class. He told the Hartford crowd that socialism would change the American government from "a political junk shop into an industrial workshop."

Germania Hall stood on Main Street, just between Morgan and Village Streets, an intersection that has long since been replaced by a highway overpass. The building was located in an area that connected downtown to the city's north end tenements. It was best known as a dance hall and meeting place for German immigrants. Bill Haywood's vision of America was heard there by hundreds of Hartford working people on that summer night, a vision that he often called "socialism with its working clothes on."

Debs, Prophet of Socialism

An eyewitness account described the speaker "moving back and forth with a stealthy pace from one side of the stage to the other, his body inclined sympathetically toward the audience, his spare long left hand resting on his hip and his sharp glance pointing into the inmost recesses of the souls present. He pictured the day when capital and labor should cease from strife and the legalized robbery of interest, rent and profit should be no more." Even the capitalist press was mesmerized by Eugene Victor Debs when he spoke at Hartford's Foot Guard Hall on June 3, 1910.

The leader of the Socialist Party had been on another stage five years earlier, flanked by Mother Jones and Lucy Parsons, when he helped found the Industrial

Workers of the World in Chicago. Anxious for the success of the One Big Union, he had even shared a speaking platform in New York City with his bitter rival Daniel DeLeon of the Socialist Labor Party in order to promote the IWW. In 1906 Debs was defending Bill Haywood in articles and speeches against Bill's frame-up murder trial in Idaho. Debs was vocal in his defense of Joe Ettor and Arturo Giovannitti, the IWW organizers wrongly accused of killing striker Anna LoPizzo in Lawrence.

By the time he reached Hartford, Debs had let his IWW membership drop. He was unhappy that the Wobblies had turned away from the political arena. He was also critical of direct action and sabotage, and openly criticized Big Bill's engagement in these tactics. In 1913 Haywood was ousted from the leadership of the Socialist Party for advocating violence, although as historian Howard Zinn notes, some of Debs' writings were far more inflammatory than anything Bill had ever said.

But the IWW was at the cutting edge of revolutionary union organizing and it had become a target of government repression. Always a principled leader, Debs knew which side he was on. "It does not matter whose fight it is, whether it be that of the IWW or AFL, the SP or the SLP, if it is a working class fight it is our fight," he wrote in 1912. "Wall Street does not fear Sammy Gompers and the AF of L [but] mortally fears the IWW," he argued.

Debs never stopped trying to bring all progressive forces together, both through union organizing and political action. He spoke in a number of Connecticut cities during this period ---including Bridgeport, Waterbury and New London—promoting the Socialist Party and its candidates for office. Although the gulf between Wobs and socialists grew over the years, Debs' ability to get votes was directly related to union growth, including IWW strength after 1910, argues David Montgomery in *The Fall of the House of Labor*. When the union movement was weakened by the concerted attacks of government and industry, Montgomery states, socialist candidates suffered as well.

In 1910 Debs stayed at the Hotel Garde on the corner of Asylum and High Streets, just a few blocks away from Foot Guard Hall. He had friends and correspondents in many cities, and in Hartford, one of them was the Congregational minister Victor L. Greenwood. Greenwood was outspoken when the socialist leader faced charges in 1918 of espionage for speaking out against World War I. Debs spent almost three years in a federal prison. It was during this time he received almost one million votes as the 1920 Socialist Party candidate for President of the United States.

The Members Are the Power

As a leader of the 1912 Willimantic strikes, Ben Legere publicly challenged John Golden to a debate about the merits of narrow craft unionism practiced by Golden's United Textile Workers (UTW). Golden had played a disreputable role in the Lawrence textile strike and spent a good amount of time and energy trying to sabotage IWW organizing efforts in textile towns throughout in Connecticut and the east coast. Ironically, before the IWW started winning in the textile industry, the UTW had ignored the pleas of immigrant mill workers to unionize.

Legere addressed the Willimantic workers after the Quidnick and American Thread workers' victory:

"The Industrial Workers of the World do not shake hands with the bosses and never will. This fight for the uplifting of humanity is no pink teas engagement or afternoon party, it's your class against the bosses. Under the present system the bosses do not want to give you a chance for advancement. They do not want you, if they can help it, to educate yourself as you should by the reading of books and other literature on modern economics.

"I was much surprised to learn on returning to Willimantic that certain persons since the grand meeting last week, had by falsehoods concerning the I.W.W. sown seeds of dissension in the ranks of the members. Efforts have and are being made to have our members break away and join craft unions. This and other movements have got the people all at sea. The members have a right to know about our organization and I am here, glad to explain. Give us a chance, don't accept all you see in the papers about the action of the organization.

"[Explaining a recent alleged desecration of the American flag in New York City] That evening there were two parades, the Industrial Workers of the World and the Italian Socialist Federation. Both had their finishing point at Union Square. The I.W.W. had a platform there from which speeches were to be made. The I.W.W. speakers and committee had their places on the platform when some of the Italian Socialist Federation men attempted to get on the platform. Whether they thought they had a right to do so is being determined. There resulted a scuffle and the table that was draped with the American flag was overturned and in that way was trampled on. The reporters working on the newspapers that are published in the interests of the bosses were on the "job" and sent the story broadcast, a deliberate lie laid to the I.W.W. People within a few feet of the stand did not notice the incident and were surprised at the story.

This, fellow workers, is a sample of what the capitalistic press is doing to hurt our cause.

"The bosses of the American Thread Company have learned a lesson. They promised you a ten per cent raise in wages. You did not get it. You went out. You sent for me and with the other I.W.W. leaders we helped you win your just demands.

"It is well to be ever watchful and not allow yourself to be oppressed. When the strike committee called on the officials of the thread company they tried to assure the committee of their benevolent intentions and considerations for their welfare and tried to explain that they had done the very best they could and proudly pointed to the fact that in some cases they had actually brought the wages up to the standard that prevailed eight years ago. Such a benevolence, with the increased cost of living during the past eight years.

"Workmen and employers have nothing in common. Under the present system they never will and for any person who thinks so, there is no place in the I.W.W. for them. The I.W.W. believes as the Socialists do, that all should share in the profits of their labors and do away with the wage system. The craft unions leaders ask for a fair day's pay for a fair day's work. Pray what does that mean to the mill owner? It means this: All that they can get out of you for the least they can pay you. The craft unions have outlived their usefulness. They may do a little for one branch of workers but what is needed is to help the masses and that is being done by the I.W.W.

"In reading the *Chronicle* of Saturday's issue that John Golden spent the greater part of the forenoon with the bosses of the Windham Silk Company. When such a man acts for the working class, goes hobnobbing with bosses, the results are no good. He is not much better than the bosses. Don't trust any trade organizer. The Textile Workers of America is well called "John Golden's Union." He wields the power. His word is law from which there is no appeal. The I.W.W. is different. The members are the power. What has John Golden accomplished? The Textile Workers of America have been organized for years and at the present time in New England have but 15,000 members. In the past seven months the Industrial Workers of the World have enrolled 50,000 members in New England, proving the strength of our organization.

"The meaning of the three stars on our union buttons stand for three noble things: Organization, Education, and Emancipation. The red flag is known the world over as the symbol of the workingman.

"In Lawrence, workers were clubbed by police while parading the streets peacefully and carrying the flag of our country at their head. The strikers offered no resistance. I hope that if anything of the kind happens in Willimantic, the members would show the same fortitude to your cause and respect to the flag that your compatriots did in Lawrence."

Defend Those Who Fought the Battle

After the IWW victories in Willimantic, the union's dynamic young organizer Elizabeth Gurley Flynn visited the Thread City on May 1st to congratulate workers there. She urged them to maintain a strong internal organization and counseled vigilance against employer retribution:

"Fellow workers, your victorious strike has been a grand one. You are here this evening to organize. Your victory must be backed up. Unless you keep up your organization you will sooner or later fail.

"It was unity on your part that ended the difficulty. It was the quickest settlement I ever heard of. The stockholders of the American Thread Company who live in Boston, Chicago, New York and other places had no other decision but grant the ten per cent raise asked. They were forced to it by a just demand. They did not care to stop their mills because of the fear of losing big dividend and in this respect their pocketbooks would be touched.

ELIZABETH FLYNN (MRS. J.A. JONES)

"On this beautiful May Day you operatives of the American Thread Company have much to be thankful for. You have won a moral as well as a labor victory in your strike for better wages and conditions. May 1 is recognized all over industrial Europe as the real labor day. By your action you have added a new spirit of independence to your lives.

"There is a new era beginning for textile workers in this country. There is no reason why you should not share in the good things in life. It is a certainty that the mill owner makes as much from the labor of this class of operatives as the mine owner, the brewers and other lines of business who have raised wages and lessened working hours.

"The day is coming when there will be an eight-hour working day and a $3 daily wage for the textiles worker. Then the real cause of broken homes will be cured. Little children can attend the schools instead of stunting their lives in the mills. Mothers will have a chance to perform what the Almighty allotted them, the care of the homes instead of trying to eke out an existence under present conditions. The bread-winner, the father, will then perform the work and the homes will be more like heaven and there will be a contented lot of people.

"When the strike committee waited on Mr. Boss and when a settlement was reached he was asked if he or the company would hold any grievance against the leaders of the strike. He stated there would be none. There were men and women in this fight and at some time there may be an attempt to weed them out. You must defend those who fought the battle."

Willimantic Resolution in Support of Ettor and Giovannitti

As the Willimantic mill workers were savoring their victory and recognizing their collective power, they began to look beyond their own circumstances to the struggles beyond their town borders. One such fight centered on trumped-up murder charges against Arturo Giovannitti and Joe Ettor, both of whom played key roles in the successful Lawrence strike. The *Willimanitc Chronicle* reprinted a resolution the Willimantic Wobblies passed to support the imprisoned organizers at the mass meeting with Gurley Flynn on May 1ˢᵗ:

Whereas, our brothers and sisters who work in the mills of Lawrence were forced by the fierce opposition of the mill owners to go on strike for more wages and better conditions, and

Whereas, when without organization to the number of 25,000 they walked out of the mills, they sent to New York for organizers to come and help them conduct their strike, Joseph J. Ettor and Arthur Giovannitti answered their call, and went to Lawrence where with all the forces of the mill owners working against, they did noble work in organizing and peacefully conducting this great strike, and

Whereas, when in a riot caused we believe by thugs in the pay of mill owners, a woman striker was shot and killed the authorities of Lawrence arrested our fellow workers, Ettor and Giovannitti and charged them with being accessories before the fact of this murder, and

Whereas, we believe that to make such a charge against these noble and unselfish men, who at the time were two miles away, and who at all times did all in their power to preserve peace and order in Lawrence, is the most infamous outrage that has ever been perpetrated against the working men of America, and

Whereas, not only have they been thrown in jail in this outrageous way but in spite of the fact that many men charged with more serious crimes in Massachusetts have been admitted to bail, your court has steadily refused to allow our fellow workers to be released on bail until their trial and has kept them in solitary confinement, therefore be it

Resolved, that we, the mill workers of Willimantic, Connecticut, in mass meeting assembled, most emphatically demand that our fellow workers, Ettor & Giovannitti be immediately released on bail, and be it further

Resolved, that we hereby serve notice that unless this demand of ours be granted, we will unite with all other mill workers in New England and in the country to bring about a great general strike until they and all other imprisoned mill workers are set free.

Blessed Are the Rebels

Months after the Bread and Roses strike had been won in March, 1912, Joe Ettor and Arturo Giovannitti were still fighting for their lives. Ettor, as the lead IWW organizer, skillfully directed the large strike committee along with Giovannitti of the Italian Socialist Federation. Although Giovannitti had worked as a coal miner, railroad laborer, and had studied to be a priest after emigrating from Italy, he was as much a poet as an organizer. "Blessed are the rebels," this former seminarian told Lawrence strikers at a mass rally, "for they shall reconquer the earth."

They were both arrested as accessories after the fact in the murder of striker Anna LoPizzo who died during a police attack on January 29th. Also jailed was striker Joseph Caruso. The men remained in a Salem, Massachusetts jail for ten months. Their arrest on "inciting to riot leading to the loss of life" was ludicrous; both organizers were miles from the scene at the time of the shooting. Their imprisonment caused outrage across the country.

In Connecticut, the Italian American community and IWW supporters mobilized to publicize the case and raise funds for their legal defense. According to the working class newspaper *Il Proletario*, May Day gatherings in West Hartford and Meriden featured speakers on the case and pledges of financial support.

In August, Robert Rives La Monte spoke to a crowd of 1,000 workers, denouncing the organizers' imprisonment and calling for a general strike if the court found them guilty. The resolution approved by the rally asserted that "we serve notice that their conviction… will be the signal for the stoppage of every wheel, machine and mill in Waterbury to remain motionless until their release." The general strike idea caught the imaginations of many. Ultimately, thousands of Lawrence workers briefly walked off their jobs in solidarity with Ettor and Giovannitti.

On August 25th in Naugatuck, IWW Local 77 held a fundraising picnic in Linen Park for the defense. Torrington was the site of another picnic and rally on September 8th. Connecticut's Matilda Rabinowitz and Ben Legere participated in many defense activities, including as featured speakers at a rally in Springfield, Massachusetts.

The trial of Ettor and Giovannitti began on September 30th. All three defendants were found not guilty on November 26th. Joe Caruso told a reporter that he hadn't even been an IWW member at the time of his arrest, but now that he was released, he was going to join up. For many Connecticut workers, the victory may not have convinced them that the legal system was fair, but it did show them of the power of their cause.

Take Their Clubs Away & Give Them Shovels

Two months after his acquittal, Giovannitti was invited to address the Italian Socialist Federation in New Haven on January 24, 1913. As usual, police were in the audience to monitor the organizer's speech:

"Within the next year the United States will face a great labor crisis which will be unlike any previous labor trouble. Discontent has been sweeping rapidly all over the country and it is a very significant fact, the strike of the 150,000 tailors in New York City and the waiters strike there also.

"The next thing which we expect to see in this country is a terrible strike in the steel industries of Pennsylvania which will be the greatest labor war that the world has ever known. The men employed in this industry and in the great steel foundries will rise and protest against the treatment which they are now receiving.

"To secure our rights in this country we must work together. Craft unionism has outlived its usefulness and with this we cannot expect to cope with the present day situation and defeat the great capitalists of this country. The place which craft unionism once occupied will be taken by industrial unionism, one big union of all workers.

"Recently they accused Ettor of having advised the striking waiters in New York to place poison in the soup which they were to serve in the fashionable New York hotels. This is untrue. If we are anxious to do away with the capitalists we'll simply refuse to work for them and starve them out. Then we'll make a pair of good longshoremen out of Mr. Morgan and Mr. Rockefeller.

"They kept Ettor and I in jail during those long ten months but they couldn't do anything to myself nor to Ettor. It was not the fault of the judge who released us, or the work of the jury nor was it the fine work of our lawyers. But it was the protests of the working class of the country that secured us our liberty. We had the press, the capitalists, and all of the monied people against us, but they could not convict us.

"I see three officers of the law standing in the rear of the room at the present time. The time will come, however, when we will take the uniforms and clubs away, place shovels in their hands, and set them to work."

Red Emma

One of the most dangerous women in America spoke in Hartford on February 12, 1913. "Red Emma" Goldman talked about love and marriage, a subject that was as revolutionary as the anarchist theory she is known for today.

It was as a Connecticut garment worker in 1888 that Goldman studied anarchist thought. She was working in a New Haven corset factory at the time. In 1890 she briefly started a dressmaking cooperative in that city and established herself as an organizer among German, Russian and Jewish immigrants.

In New York, young Emma met Alexander Berkman, whose "propaganda of the deed" led him in 1892 to try to kill industrialist Henry Clay Frick during the Homestead steelworkers strike in which workers were murdered by Pinkerton agents. Berkman failed and landed a twenty-year jail sentence. Goldman defended the man who was to become her life partner, which left her isolated from many allies and often forced her to live in parks and whore houses. One year later she was in jail herself on the trumped up charge of "inciting to riot." There she worked as a nurse's aide in the prison hospital. By 1897, her reputation as an agitator and theorist had been established, and soon after Emma Goldman was touring throughout New England, across the country and in Europe.

Goldman raised funds for the Lawrence textile strikers in 1912 and became friendly with Bill Haywood and Elizabeth Gurley Flynn. She defended the IWW activists who spearheaded the San Diego Free Speech fight, ignoring her own safety. It was during this time that her companion Ben Reitman was kidnapped by vigilantes, tortured and branded with "IWW" on his back. From the proceeds donated at her public meetings, Goldman and others set up a "feeding station" that provided clothes and food from sympathetic shop keepers.

She published "Marriage and Love" in 1911. The pamphlet analyzed how the social institution of marriage maintained capitalism. Derided as an advocate of "free love" for her view against compulsory monogamy, Goldman responded "Free love? As if love is anything but free it can live in no other atmosphere. In freedom it gives itself unreservedly, abundantly, completely." Marriage, on the other hand, "incapacitates [a woman] for life's struggle, annihilates her social consciousness, paralyzes her imagination."

The fact that authorities allowed Emma Goldman to speak anywhere in Hartford should not be taken for granted. She was probably kicked out of more U.S. cities than any other human being. The New Haven police admitted her into a lecture hall in 1909, but they kept out all the people who came to see her. In Burlington Vermont, the mayor stopped her from a public appearance. In El Paso Texas, she was allowed to speak in English, but not in Spanish. Goldman spent several decades in standoffs with police, fighting to simply express her ideas.

More than 500 people crowded into Hartford's Columbia Hall to hear this woman and her dangerous ideas. Goldman was accompanied by her longtime partner Alexander Berkman, by then freed from prison. She told the enthusiastic Hartford audience that "in love only comes the divine union between men and women, and the sanction of the church or law cannot make it a bit more sacred or holy."

Emma Goldman spent her life in struggle—and much more time in jail—by advocating birth control and opposing World War I. By 1919, she was deported to Russia, under the direction of a young government agent who was making a name for himself by attacking "reds." Emma Goldman was labeled "one of the most dangerous women in America" by J. Edgar Hoover, who personally supervised her deportation, and who never did get married.

Looking the World Straight in the Eye

By the time Helen Keller reached Hartford in April, 1913, she was a card-carrying member of the IWW. Keller was without sight or hearing but during her lifetime she opened the eyes of millions to poverty and oppression, and she obliged the public to listen to the Wobblies' revolutionary ideas.

As a child Keller became a celebrity, or maybe a curiosity, for overcoming the disabilities caused by scarlet fever when she was barely two years old. When she was fourteen, Keller traveled to New York City's slums and began to think critically about how society treated its most vulnerable people. "I have visited sweatshops, factories, crowded slums of New York and Washington," she explained in an interview. "Of course I could not see the squalor; but if I could not see it, I could smell it. With my own hands I could feel pinched, dwarfed children tending their younger brothers and sisters, while their mothers tended machines in nearby factories."

When she was about twenty years old, Keller enrolled at Radcliffe College and met John Macy, a man who became a pivotal figure in her life. She was introduced to socialism by Macy, a Harvard instructor who eventually married Annie Sullivan, Helen's longtime teacher. By 1909, Keller was recruited by the

Socialist Party (SP) and began reading the Braille versions of Marx and other theorists in English, German and French.

Keller became impatient with the incremental parliamentary strategy of the Socialists, writing in the *New York Tribune* that the Party was "sinking into a political bog." It was losing its revolutionary character "as it occupies a place under the government and seeks office under it." The Lawrence strike transformed her: "I discovered that the true idea of the IWW is not only to better conditions, to get them for all people, but to get them at once."

She moved to Wrentham, Massachusetts with Annie and John. It was at their home that a number of famous activists including Arturo Giovannitti found respite and a hostess eager to learn. The friendship that formed during those visits led Keller to write the introduction to *Arrows in the Gale,* Giovannitti's book of poetry published by Hillacre Bookhouse in the Riverside section of Westport, Connecticut. Hillacre promoted the works of Lincoln Steffens, Oscar Wilde and other radical and avant garde thinkers of the time. Helen wrote of Giovannitti that "as a poet he is to be judged by his success in rendering [his] ideas in verse, and not by his relations to Syndicalism or Socialism or any movement in which he happens to be active."

The Italian organizer's political outlook is obvious from his subject matter: workers, hoboes, poor children, prostitutes, political prisoners all feature prominently. One poem is a tribute to Joe Ettor, Giovannitti's fellow organizer and cell mate. It was written while both men were in prison and on trial for their lives. The poem makes it clear that Giovannitti expected a death sentence for being falsely accused of the murder of Lawrence striker Anna LoPizzo.

As Keller learned more about the union, she risked her reputation and her livelihood to speak out. She defended Bill Haywood, Gene Debs, Joe Hill and other Wobs, all targets of government attacks. "I love them for their needs, their miseries, their endurance and their daring spirit," Keller told a New York crowd. "Their cause is my cause. While they are threatened and imprisoned, I am manacled."

As celebrated as she was, fame did not pay Helen Keller's bills. She began her first speaking tour in February, 1913 at the age of thirty-two. On April 4 she arrived in Hartford. This "bread and butter" presentation covered her personal struggle to communicate with the world, an inspiring victory due largely to the work of Annie Sullivan. Mark Twain called Keller one of the "two most interesting characters" of the century (the other being Napoleon). "The men and women who crowded into Unity Hall last night to see Miss Helen Keller felt that they had witnessed a miracle even greater than they expected" wrote a *Hartford Courant* reporter. Her tour took place under the auspices of the Junior Republic, a charity formed in New York for "neglected or wayward children."

Keller was dogged by criticism of her politics wherever she traveled. Soon after her speech, the *Courant* complained that she was being manipulated by radicals and implied she was a hypocrite for taking donations from wealthy capitalists. At least one Connecticut reader disagreed. "She has remarkable powers of penetration," replied T.A. Ryan, "which coupled with a sublime sympathy for that portion of humanity which suffers ... have caused her to place herself on record as being in favor of abolishing this unjust system. She knows there is but one remedy—Socialism—to cure the cancer which is slowly destroying the body politic and so has ardently espoused that philosophy." Keller maintained her radical views for many years despite the widespread criticism from the mainstream press. She raised money for IWW members during a mass trial in Chicago. She supported relief efforts for Republican Spain and maintained a lasting friendship with Elizabeth Gurley Flynn. She opposed the witch hunts against progressives by Senator Joseph McCarthy in the 1940s.

In 1938 Helen moved to Westport, Connecticut, not far from the small publishing house that had printed Giovannitti's book. By that time, the FBI had been maintaining a secret file on her for thirteen years. One entry concerns a letter she sent to J. Edgar Hoover requesting a donation for an international relief effort she supported. It was a form letter, Hoover sniffed, so he would not acknowledge it. Helen Keller may have been thinking of Hoover when she wrote "the only thing worse than being blind is having sight but no vision."

The Dangerous Proposition

Harry Hardy traveled from Boston to the borough of Shelton, Connecticut with a mission: stop IWW organizer Matilda Rabinowitz. He brought with him other employees of the Sherman Detective Agency, ready to break the strike of more than 1,000 weavers and mill workers at Sidney Blumenthal & Company, a strike organized by the Wobblies on November 12, 1913.

Hardy offered to use the same techniques his agency had developed in Massachusetts. At a Brockton shoe strike his men had insinuated themselves into the union leadership, won posts as treasurer and strike secretary, bankrupted the union's efforts, and forced the shoemakers back to work.

This time, however, Harry Hardy had an even better idea. Strike organizer Matilda Rabinowitz was a "dangerous proposition." Hardy and his men would kidnap her, depriving the workers of their young charismatic leader. The scheme was never carried out; word leaked that Matilda was the target of the planned abduction. She briefly noted it in her report to the IWW headquarters.

Matilda Rabinowitz (born Tatania Gitel Rabinowitz in 1887 in Ukrainia) emigrated to New York at the age of thirteen. Soon her family moved to Stamford and later to Bridgeport. She worked in shirtwaist and corset factories, millinery and department stores, in a private nursery and as a nursing home aide. Other working class factory girls labored long hours for low pay in dangerous jobs without ever having the opportunity to challenge their lot in life, but Rabinowitz was different. She identified the capitalist system as the source of women workers' suffering, and she decided to take action.

By the time she was in her early twenties, Rabinowitz had joined the socialist movement. She took a job with the Connecticut Industrial Commission and moved to Hartford, interviewing factory workers about their conditions. During this time she considered going to college, but the union movement proved to be a stronger attraction. Rabinowitz's growing desire for justice led her first to the American Federation of Labor (AFL), which she soon discovered cared little about the plight of unskilled working women. The AFL's indifference pushed her toward the IWW.

Matilda Rabinowitz's first union experience was in the 1912 Lawrence strike, where her energy and competence caught the attention of the IWW's leaders. She traveled back and forth from Massachusetts to Connecticut, raising money for the strike from Bridgeport workers. After the historic Lawrence victory, Matilda was asked by the IWW's Vincent St. John to travel to Little Falls, New York. The textile struggle there honed her strike skills. Organizing soup kitchens, speaking to supporters, and raising funds did not make headlines, but her work played the critical role in keeping up the strikers' strength and morale. After strike leader Benjamin Legere went to jail, she led the strikers in a mass meeting and victory march.

In 1913, Rabinowitz made an extraordinary journey across Michigan, Ohio, and Pennsylvania, working on IWW strikes at silk mills, automobile plants, steel mills and cigar factories. In each of these union drives, she was the only woman organizer. Despite the fact that so many female-dominated industries were ripe for organizing, Matilda and Elizabeth Gurley Flynn were the only women paid by the IWW as organizers during this period.

When the boss at Blumenthal cut wages in November, 1913, it was the spark the union needed. Rabinowitz, back from her travels, met with the workers and immediately sent a telegram to *Solidarity*, the IWW's newspaper. It was brief, like all such messages, but its tone was urgent, reflecting her excitement and determination: "Four hundred weavers out in Blumenthal Company's plant, Shelton. All joined organization. More coming: expect to tie up mill."

Matilda Rabinowitz organized a strong strike committee that was "planning to give the mill owners a hard fight ... until victory is achieved" she pledged. Their demands included the ten-hour day, abolition of forced overtime, and a weekly pay system. The workers also insisted on an increase in the piece rate, and a certain level of security for weavers when their looms broke down. Breakdowns were not the weaver's fault, they argued, and they shouldn't lose pay because of it. The committee demanded a daily minimum wage of $3.00.

Early in the strike Blumenthal had taken out full page ads to demonstrate that his weavers were well-paid. Matilda Rabinowitz replied that the company's figures were misleading, since they did not include the slow months when work was scarce, and that only a select group of higher-waged men were listed.

Maintaining the day-to-day organizing was not an easy task. Rabinowitz battled not only bosses and hostile business leaders, she was forced to challenge the prejudices that some of the strikers had against immigrant workers whose religion or ethnicity differed from theirs. Perhaps this is why the young Russian Jew later adopted the Americanized surname Robbins. She made no such accommodation, however, while she organized in the Naugatuck Valley.

She threw herself into the efforts to maintain solidarity, speaking every day to the strikers in Russian, Yiddish, and English. Forced to meet outside of Shelton, she hired local halls in nearby Derby and Ansonia. The organizer encouraged local grocers to increase their prices and share the profits with the strikers. No one could help notice Rabinowitz as she led marches down Main Street. "Her petite form looked odd among the stalwart men," wrote one newspaper reporter.

On January 12 1914, the strikers rallied at the Sterling Opera House in Derby. The meeting was chaired by Michael Dumas, an IWW leader and a weaver at the Specialty Weaving Company of Shelton. Earlier in the year, Dumas had led a strike that failed to reach its objectives but had built IWW Local 528 and maintained a strong presence in the plant. Specialty's owner tried to fire Dumas during the course of the Blumenthal strike, but his co-workers staged their own walk-out and protected their leader's job.

Arturo Giovannitti was the featured speaker at the Opera House. "You can't win anything by staying home to sleep or by reading your Bible over again," he told the crowd. "That's all very well but it doesn't win strikes."

Rabinowitz was the big hit of the rally. The idea that a woman might actually be an effective organizer of male textile workers was unusual; she was consistently described in the press as "frail," "diminutive," and "of girlish appearance." But no one could deny that she spoke with great force and the power of her convictions:

"I apologize to the people of Shelton who came here out of curiosity. I fear the IWW speakers here tonight have disappointed you. None of them have come to the stage with a stiletto in his teeth. They carry no guns, nor do they bring with them bombs with sputtering fuses. My aim is not to speak to those who exploit but to those who are exploited. I am not concerned with what is the reputation of the IWW in these parts. It makes not a particle of difference to me whether they like me in Shelton or not. With this revolutionary movement we recognize no country and we recognize no flag. The foreigner and the American are brothers in the misery and degradation and terrible sufferings of poverty. John Brown went to the gallows. He was sent there by the same respectable mob, if you please, that says in Shelton and in Derby that the IWW organizer ought to be tarred and feathered and run out of town. But if I am taken out of Shelton today, six or eight or ten or twelve others will come here. And if they are driven out of town, there will be a hundred to take their places."

Rabinowitz anticipated that the Blumenthal boss would use all the forces at his disposal to beat the strike. What she had not expected was the betrayal by local socialist leader Samuel Beardsley. During the first week of the Blumenthal strike, Beardsley distributed flyers warning strikers (in five languages!) that picket line violence was a violation of state law. His action exacerbated an already tense situation. Blumenthal hired the notorious O'Brien detective agency to patrol the factory. The O'Briens were founded by Boss Farley, described by the *New York Times* as the "king strike breaker who developed the business into a science."

Every move Beardsley made seemed to be designed to undermine the IWW's efforts while maintaining an outward appearance of support. According to Rabinowitz, he had a spy in the strike committee who would report to him every night. Then Beardsley and other Socialist Party members would contact strike leaders individually to try and convince them to return to work. Beardsley even had himself appointed to a borough-sponsored "settlement committee" made up of prominent men. The committee interviewed Blumenthal and determined that he would never deal with the IWW. Beardsley was also behind a rumor, Matilda Rabinowitz believed, that she was mismanaging the strike's finances. In a union report, the Wobbly organizer wrote that Beardsley had been "carrying on against the IWW in the dark, using true Tammany Hall methods."

Sam Beardsley served as Connecticut state secretary of the Socialist Party. He had championed a change to the party's national constitution in 1912, known as Section 6, which banned any member who "advocates crime, sabotage, or other methods of violence." Beardsley and his comrades won that fight, which led to the expulsion from the Party of many Wobblies and leader Bill Haywood. In fact, no Wobbly organizer had ever been convicted of sabotage, as confirmed in 1939 by a Johns Hopkins University investigation. Beardsley boasted to the Blumenthal strikers that he had helped pass Section 6, a clear message that he believed Shelton would be better off without the IWW.

Shelton's burgesses, the equivalent of town councilmen, paid massive overtime to keep local police on duty, spending up to $200 a day. The O'Brien detectives earned a minimum of $25 a day. Weavers, by contrast, had been making about $7 a week when work was available.

Blumenthal also put the O'Briens inside the mill and outfitted them with beds and gas stoves. For the Blumenthal Company and Shelton's town fathers, this fight was not just about money. It was about power, and Sidney Blumenthal intended to keep control of his mill at any cost.

Although the strikers became increasingly restless, their hostility was only sporadic toward the scabs imported from other cities and the thugs who protected them. Violence from the police and the detectives, by contrast, was constant and ferocious. The O'Briens would "insult and aggravate the strikers in many ways," according to a news report, while the IWW strikers "desire to conduct themselves peaceably."

For her part, Rabinowitz cautioned the mill workers against anything that would distract them from proper strike conduct. "I am not a Prohibitionist," she told IWW men in one of her daily talks. "I don't insist that men must be total abstainers. But in a time like this, men with strong drink are led to do things that they ought not to do. Let the strike breakers and the guards do the drinking. We must get along without it."

Despite the public criticism of Matilda Rabinowitz in the press and the treacherous undercurrent fomented by Comrade Beardsley, the strikers were not about to abandon the 26-year old organizer who had stood by them every step of the way. At one point, she offered to resign if the strikers thought it would be in their best interests. Hundreds of men responded with a "rousing demonstration of confidence."

Sidney Blumenthal's assault on the strike was unrelenting, and he had help from elements of the AFL. Blumenthal not only hired scabs from Bridgeport, Providence and Philadelphia, but had striking AFL plumbers shipped in from New Haven. He even convinced the Massachusetts Employment Bureau (an official state agency) to send workers to operate the idle looms. The Bureau's head, Harry Dunderdale, was also secretary of the Boston Central Labor Union.

Official violence against the strikers intensified. Police severely beat a woman because she failed to move along when ordered. An innocent bystander was clubbed by guards, who insisted the man had fallen from an automobile. Agents entered a private house, attacked and beat up two men and had them arrested because "their party was too loud." One mill guard falsely accused a local farm hand as the culprit who tossed a stone through a saloon window. In response, the bartender beat the elderly farmer, Alex Havrilla, with a pool cue. Havrilla died of his injuries. The bartender was arrested but the O'Brien guard fled across the state line to avoid prosecution.

Women played a particularly assertive role as official violence increased. They faced down the police and the O'Briens armed only with hot water or handfuls of pepper. These homemade weapons were no match for Winchester rifles and Colt revolvers. Mary Smarsh, a 38-year old widow with four small children, was shot during a melee between strikers and police. Mary's son was injured by clubs in the same battle.

The most shameful incident of violence took place eight weeks into the strike. Police dragged a couple, Michael and Carolyn Homick, from their home during a disturbance near the mill. Their children were left alone in the freezing apartment. The couple was badly beaten before being arrested. Michael was immediately sentenced to 15 days in jail; Carolyn was released but her injuries were so severe that she could not care for her two-month old child Mary. The infant, already malnourished, died three days later. The strikers organized a mass funeral procession with the child's coffin at the front of their ranks.

Samuel Beardsley and his settlement committee met inside the plant with Blumenthal and were given an IWW pamphlet that the boss said was sufficient reason to exclude Wobblies from employment. "We have done everything possible to bring about settlement of this struggle," Beardsley sadly concluded.

Over the next two days controversy erupted among the strikers. Paranoia about the IWW was growing, exacerbated by the local socialists, and there were intense debates at the strike meetings. Three votes took place on whether or not to return to work. Finally, a vote of 137 to 133 called off the strike. According to town officials, Blumenthal had agreed to a shorter work week and weekly pay envelopes, two of the strikers' original demands.

O'Brien men stayed in the plant to watch the returning workers. Blumenthal made the former strikers raise their right hands and swear they would give up their IWW cards. The machinists, all AFL members, were refused jobs because they had honored the Wobblies' picket line. Most weavers refused to return to the Blumenthal mills under the new conditions and left town to seek work elsewhere. Someone stole the union's membership book, which ended up in Blumenthal's hands.

"Let this incident in the history of labor stand out as an example of the work some of the socialist politicians are doing in the labor movement,' wrote a bitter Matilda Rabinowitz, "and the assistance they render to labor's emancipation." David Rabinowitz, Matilda's brother who had originally helped bring her into the Socialist Party, denounced Beardsley at a party meeting for betraying the

Blumenthal strike. David, who for years had been an organizer for the Socialists, was expelled from the group.

Rabinowitz left Shelton, and between 1914 and 1915, she spent five months organizing textile workers in the company town of Greenville, South Carolina. On behalf of the IWW, she traveled to this southern town with the name of only one person to contact. When she arrived, Rabinowitz set up a soapbox outside the local revival tent and soon attracted her own "converts." Now 27 years old, Rabinowitz built the first southern IWW local in the textile town.

The poverty and oppression Rabinowitz witnessed in South Carolina had a profound impact on her. In February, 1915, she published a story in the *Waterbury Herald* about the daily life of a fictional cotton mill family. The stereotyped dialect she uses does not obscure the deep empathy with which Rabinowitz sketched the hard lives she witnessed. [The story appears at the end of this book.]

Sometime after her east coast organizing, Matilda Rabinowitz became Matilda Robbins. She moved on and organized for the United Auto Workers, worked as a labor newspaper editor, and later as a social worker. She always remained a Wobbly, however, and wrote for the IWW newspaper until her death in 1963.

The Millionaire Socialist

Robert Rives La Monte was installed as a delegate at IWW's founding convention on June 28, 1905, the second day of the historic Chicago meeting. The 37-year old had trained as a lawyer and was admitted to the bar in two states, but by this time he was known as a writer and a national organizer for the Socialist Party. Apparently, the convention delegates were unaware of La Monte's legal credentials, for as they were approving him as a delegate they were simultaneously arguing *against* the admission of another attorney who had traveled from New York to participate

Although he is little known today, Connecticut's La Monte achieved prominence as a contemporary of H.L. Mencken, the pioneering journalist and editor. The two published a book in which they debated socialism and Mencken's belief in a natural aristocracy, entitled *Men vs. The Man.*

In 1908 La Monte moved to New Canaan, located just north of Stamford in wealthy Litchfield County. Although he was a world traveler, he did most of his writing from that Republican town where his wife Mary's family lived.

La Monte also gained a high profile for his political activity in Connecticut, most notably when he ran on the 1912 Socialist Party ticket for Lieutenant Governor. His running mate was Samuel Beardsley, the Bridgeport party leader who was to play such a disturbing role in the Shelton textile strike.

Unlike the conservative Beardsley, La Monte's beliefs placed him in the left wing of the Socialist Party. In an article he wrote for the *International Socialist Review* La Monte argued that no matter which political party gained power, it would support reforms like workers' compensation, unemployment insurance and pensions—none of which yet widely existed. "Modern social legislation" would actually increase profits and benefit the rich more than the poor, La Monte wrote. So, he concluded, support for the Socialist Party would lead to "revolutionary reforms," the kind that close the gap between rich and poor. Political action and union organizing had to work hand-in-hand, La Monte insisted. Socialists in office had to support the growth of "class unions" because capitalists could not be allowed to have "unimpeded control of the police, the judiciary and all the powers of political government" that worked to crush workers' organizations.

La Monte cited the most recent Socialist Party convention which had endorsed a close relationship with class conscious, industrial unions. This, of course, described the work of the IWW. But in his article La Monte failed to mention the adoption by the SP of the infamous Section 6 clause which was used to eject many Wobblies from the Party.

La Monte was at the Hartford Socialist Hall on January 28, 1912 to speak on the subject of "The Brotherhood of Man, How to Get It: Ballots Ever, Bullets Never!" His talk took place at the same exact time that Edmund Seidel, a New York state senator, spoke on "Socialism and the Church" at the rival Socialist Labor Party Hall nearby. In May, La Monte attended the Connecticut Socialist Party convention where he was selected as their candidate for Lieutenant Governor. At that meeting, the Socialists barred party members from belonging to any militia or military organization. They also sent a telegram of support to Joe Ettor and Arturo Giovannitti who were on trial after being framed for the murder of the Anna LoPizzo. The convention studiously avoided mentioning that Ettor was an IWW man. At a mass meeting in New Haven later that summer, La Monte proposed that there should be a general strike if Ettor and Giovannitti were convicted.

Nationwide, the Socialist ticket was led by Eugene Debs as its presidential candidate. He attracted 1,000 workers when he spoke in Bristol one month before the election. Debs garnered almost a million votes for president in 1912, more than he had in his 1908 bid. In Connecticut, the SP ticket won about 10,000 votes, double what they had gotten four years earlier, but still a fraction of those eligible to vote.

In 1914, war broke out in Europe. Gene Debs opposed America's entrance into the conflict, and his anti-war speeches eventually landed him in federal prison. But the World War had the opposite effect on La Monte. The New Canaan socialist dropped his SP membership and enlisted in the Connecticut Home Guard to protect, he said, his naïve pacifist neighbors. He continued to write for newspapers and magazines and ran for state representative as a Democrat in 1920.

The Lamont family traced its heritage to the first Puritans (Robert La Monte's side of the family kept the old spelling of their last name). They were wealthy, but their politics were a mixed bag. Thomas Lamont, chair of J.P. Morgan company, was called a "wealthy progressive pacifist." Other family members included Corliss Lamont, the socialist civil libertarian, and Ned Lamont, who unsuccessfully for U.S. Senate in 2006; opposition to the Iraq War is what distinguished him from his opponents.

Robert Rives La Monte was a "parlor socialist" (Mencken's term) during a time when the IWW was fighting for free speech and its members were being thrown into jail for organizing the country's disinherited majority. But as one Wobbly wrote, in a critique of socialist intellectuals of the day, "It is not the Sorels ... the Wallings, La Montes and such who count the most—it is the obscure Bill Jones on the firing line, with stink in his clothes, rebellion in his brain, hope in his heart, determination in his eyes and direct action in his gnarled fists."

Anonymous but Not Forgotten

IWW organizers traveled throughout Connecticut cities and towns, looking for the right time and place to strike a spark among the state's working men and women.

In July, 1915, Torrington officials refused when two Wobblies requested a permit for an open air meeting at Center Square. Mutao Plesca was arrested in 1917 and spent several months in jail for the "crime" for having IWW literature in his home. Germalino Seggrio, dubbed the "anarchist poet," was arrested in Ansonia in 1918 for failing to register for the draft.

The new Sedition Act provided authorities the power to arrest five young Russian workers in Bristol for possession of literature "calculated to impede the successful prosecution of the war." They were rounded up at their workplaces on June 4, 1918. Ananl Nazarachuk, Henry Veynnon, Alexander Hiskho, John Kuhhl and Efen Paleto were taken to Hartford as part of a nationwide crackdown on the distribution of "nefarious literature."

Also in Ansonia, Harry Dorsch was arrested in June, 1919 for "loitering" and handed over to federal authorities for possible deportation. Dorsch had IWW literature and a black flag in his possession, authorities declared, which was enough to connect him to recent local strikes.

But mostly, we will never know their names. In Danbury, three men were arrested for distributing IWW literature in April, 1919. They were sent to Bridgeport and handed over to federal agents. As Putnam workers at American Velvet Company struck in June, 1917, IWW organizers sought their affiliation with the one big union (they settled on the AFL instead). The Hartford Manufacturers' Association kept a watchful eye on the city's factory district and reported in July, 1919 that IWW literature was circulating among workers there. New Britain's Wobblies congregated at Skritulsky's Hall on Broad Street and had a "well-organized branch" in July, 1919, according to police.

The relentless partnership between Connecticut bosses and the legal system presented a constant challenge to IWW organizing. Anti-union methods—both legal and illegal—escalated as the tenacious Wobblies made it clear they weren't going away.

Dangerous Lawlessness

In the early morning hours of August 1, 1917, six masked men forced IWW organizer Frank Little from his boarding house in Butte, Montana. They tied him behind a car and dragged him to a railroad trestle. There he was lynched. Thousands of local miners attended his funeral, and his death had an impact as far away as Connecticut.

Frank Little, who was part Cherokee from Oklahoma, had worked for the IWW since 1906. He was a veteran of the free speech fights, including one in 1909 where he was jailed for 30 days in Spokane, Washington for reading the Declaration of Independence. Little successfully argued for the creation of the Agricultural Workers Organization (AWO) within the IWW, which became one of the union's most successful efforts. He organized fruit pickers, lumber workers and miners throughout the West. He was an outspoken critic of the war in Europe, which the United States had entered on April 6, 1917. Frank arrived in Butte three months later to organize the workers of the Anaconda Mining Company. He spoke out against the war at a mass meeting of miners on a Butte baseball field just shortly before he was murdered.

Only one day after Frank Little's death, the *Bridgeport Evening Farmer* published this editorial:

"The lynching of Frank Little at Butte is a more dangerous sign of anarchy than all the misdeeds of the I.W.W. committed since the organization came into being.

"These lynchings undoubtedly were conducted by men of substance and standing, who were angered over the labor troubles brought on by the organization of which Little was a chief.

"The necessity for peace between capital and labor is overwhelming. This peace is not a vision; it is something that can be attained. But the attainment of it is made difficult by these lawless and selfish Montana men who waste no time in thought.

"Little, however mistaken he may have been, was engaged in a collective movement. He was making personal sacrifice and running a personal risk in a cause which personally could bring him little profit.

"The men who lynched Little had no public motive. They were annoyed in their business relations. That was all.

"When they killed Little, they raised up ten opponents to them and their system, where one existed before. Property [capitalists] must not make the mistake of supposing that labor in America sympathizes with the lynchers in Butte. Labor sympathizes with the man who was lynched.

"Such things make the workers feel that the life of a worker is not safe, if he engages in any species of agitation repulsive to his superiors in wealth and position.

"Little was either keeping the law, or breaking it. If he was breaking the law, he should have been punished by the law; if he was not breaking the law his person should have been as safe in Butte as the person of any other man.

"The president, in the interest of American institutions, in the behalf of good feeling between capital and labor, should see to it that the Butte lynchers are found and punished. Their crime was murder. They are dangerous anarchists. They are inciting the people. They are stimulating lawlessness. They are playing a game in which the forces of law and order, and the stability of property and the rights of man are sure to lose."

Frank Little's killers were never brought to justice.

FRANK LITTLE
VICTIM OF ANACONDA COPPER CO THUGS
DIED AUG 1, 1917 BUTTE MONT

Mistaken Identity

Sergeant Mullings thought he recognized the famous Italian American labor agitator when he stepped off the train in Ansonia. As the man began to address a crowd of strikers at the corner of Maple and High Streets, Mullings arrested him. The city was now safe from IWW leader Joe Ettor, and the police officer was congratulated for his quick action. The *Waterbury American* ran a story of the capture with Ettor's photo on the front page.

Actually, the arrested organizer wasn't Ettor at all. The police had apprehended Fred Biedenkapp, a German-American official of the Brotherhood of Metal Workers. But paranoia about the IWW was running high during June, 1919, ever since a general strike in Waterbury had spread through the Naugatuck Valley.

Sergeant Mullings mistook Biedenkapp for "Smiling Joe" Ettor, a Brooklyn-born IWW organizer who spoke four languages. His success as a leader of the 1912 Lawrence textile strike made him one of the country's most prominent Wobblies. But his comments during the 1913 New York waiters' strike were what really set off hysteria in Connecticut.

According to press reports, Joe told a mass meeting of waiters that if they went back to work without their demands being met, restaurant and hotel owners should know that "it is the unsafest proposition in the world for the capitalists to eat food prepared and served by members of your union."

Opponents of the IWW seized on this quote to start a furious campaign against Ettor. An editorial in the *New Haven Times Leader* called his speech an "open instigation to murder." Emma Goldman was imprisoned for less, the paper argued. In New York, business leaders tried to have Ettor indicted for his rhetoric.

It did not matter to the authorities that Joe Ettor was not a violent man. In fact, he was credited with maintaining the peace among the Lawrence strikers in the face of massive police provocation and violence. His leadership there brought "a policy of non-resistance to the aggressions of the police and militia" according to a contemporary observer.

The Italian-language newspaper *Corriere del Connecticut* offered a different version of the Wobbly's New York speech. "Ettor intended to talk about food rendered impossible to eat but not poisoned," the paper reported, referring to the tactic of spoiling a meal and then serving it. During the waiters' strike, Arturo Giovannitti suggested adding large amounts of salt to customers' food to make it inedible.

Two weeks after the incident, Joe was invited to New Haven by the Italian Socialist Federation. He couldn't attend because he was traveling to Tacoma, Washington to visit his sick father. Giovannitti took his place and addressed the enthusiastic audience.

Even though the Ansonia cop had been wrong about Joe Ettor's arrival, the organizer *had* spent time in Connecticut a few years earlier, staying at Walnut Beach in Milford. He had also addressed a meeting of Italian workers in Waterbury on September 1, 1915. At the event Ettor spotted a plainclothes detective in the audience and demanded he leave. Seven cops raided the hall in response, and nearly started a riot. They arrested Ettor for breach of peace and interfering with a police officer. After he posted bond, Waterbury detectives kept Ettor under surveillance.

Ettor was found guilty and sentenced to six months in jail. He appealed the verdict to District Court, where a deal was struck to have the sentence suspended providing he leave town and never return. Joe Ettor knew there were many other cities to organize.

The Revolution is Not a Tea Party

The Willimantic Wobbly had just turned 26 when he was convicted on riot charges during the Little Falls textile strike in New York. But the frame-up did not stop him from organizing workers, as the authorities had desperately hoped. Once he began a year-long sentence at the nearby Auburn prison in 1913, Ben Legere became a teacher at the prison school. Always the organizer, this young writer and activist taught other inmates about industrial unionism and revolutionary socialism, right under the warden's nose.

Benjamin James Legere was born in Taunton, Massachusetts on May 30, 1887, the same year Albert Parsons and the other Haymarket martyrs were hanged. "When they executed the Chicago anarchists, Legere came on the scene," he once said. "So, serves them right, huh?"

His father was French-Canadian and part Micmac (Mi'kmaq) Indian who worked his way from Canada to New York, getting jobs as a logger, iron worker and finally, as a small farmer in Massachusetts. When son Ben was 19 years old, he joined the Brotherhood of Railway Clerks, "under the impression I was joining a genuine labor union," he later wrote. He found, however, that the union "was being used by the railroad companies to keep the clerks from organizing." The BRC was "in reality an organization machine carefully controlled by the companies."

As a young man, Legere was an aspiring actor and playwright. Two of his plays, both socially topical, were produced locally to positive reviews (although the Mayor of Taunton tried to shut down Legere's play *The Reformer*). His theater skills would ultimately be put to good use as a union organizer.

Legere moved to Bridgeport around 1909 and quickly hooked up with the Socialist Party, speaking on street corners, chairing public meetings, and running for the city's Board of Alderman on the Socialist ticket. By the next year he was the chair of the adjustment board of the Railway Clerks union, trying to settle disputes between workers and their boss. Soon after, he became an active member of the Bridgeport Socialist Club, a smaller and more militant rival to the electoral-minded Socialist Party chapter led at the time by Samuel Beardsley. It was here in the "Park City" that Legere met Matilda Rabinowitz, who was the same age and also an SP member. They became movement partners and eventually lovers, though Ben Legere already had a wife and family.

Socialist activity led them both to the IWW. By 1911 Legere was helping to launch a local of the Brotherhood of Machinists in Bridgeport along with Bill Haywood and Elizabeth Gurley Flynn. In early 1912 he and Rabinowitz were

COMRADE BEN J. LEGERE.

raising funds for the Bread and Roses strike. Together they prepared to place Lawrence strikers' children in the homes of Bridgeport families as part of the famous children's exodus. Legere was active up in Lawrence, too. He crashed a City Hall meeting where the bosses were stirring up anti-IWW sentiment, at a considerable threat to his own safety. "He came out all right, thanks to his calmness under the circumstances," reported the IWW's Justus Ebert.

Legere harshly criticized the Bridgeport Socialist Party leadership for its lack of effort on behalf of the Lawrence strikers. The party finally offered a city council resolution of "moral support" after the strike had essentially been won. "The workers in Lawrence needed no moral support," Legere wrote, "their cause is so unquestionably just and moral in every way that to offer them moral support is bitter irony."

In May, Legere was in Willimantic helping to lead the successful Quidnick and American Thread Company mill strikes. Both fights had been inspired by the recent victory of the Lawrence workers. It was here he challenged AFL textile union leader John Golden to a debate on industrial unionism versus craft unionism. Golden had played a treacherous role in Lawrence and again in Willimantic, undermining the IWW's efforts and colluding with the bosses. "Defend yourself on the charge that you are a disorganizer of labor instead of a labor organizer," Legere wrote to Golden on May 12th. Golden did not respond but held his own meeting at Town Hall, which city officials would not rent to the Wobblies. Across town the IWW organized a rally featuring Legere and Elizabeth Gurley Flynn. It attracted three times as many Willimantic workers as Golden's event. Meanwhile, the police and local authorities did their best to break up street meetings by Legere and other IWW leaders. The Wobs resisted the public speaking ban; by August, Ben Legere was speaking to an "open-air mass meeting" of at least 500 workers in Willimantic's Lincoln Square. Up until this time Legere self-identified as an industrial union socialist. Now he was a full-fledged Wobbly.

By the fall of 1912, Legere announced that he was establishing a statewide IWW office in the Thread City. It would not be staffed by him for long. He worked nonstop to help free the imprisoned Ettor and Giovannitti. Legere traveled as far as the Paper Makers' union hall in Livermore Falls Maine, some 300 miles north of Bridgeport, to promote the IWW and the impending trial.

Just before the strike leaders' acquittal, Ben and Matilda were called to the mill workers' strike at Little Falls, New York. He was arrested on November 1st along with at least a dozen strikers and organizer Philip Bocchino when the authorities broke up a peaceful union rally at the Phoenix textile mill. The IWW spectacle had all the earmarks of a Legere production: women strikers were dressed in red sweaters; the marching band played La Marseillaise. The police stopped the assembly in the park and then physically broke up the march. The town fathers were determined to disrupt the strike by attacking its leaders and smearing the Wobblies as violent radicals. A private detective was stabbed and a police officer was shot during the melee. Police witnesses charged that Legere and Bocchino were responsible.

Ben Legere escaped during the police riot, thanks to the aid of some strikers. He soon came forward, however, to face the trumped up charges and a kangaroo trial. The wounded detective later admitted he had lied about Legere attacking him. Legere and Bocchino were still found guilty of inciting to riot on May 19, 1913 and sent to the Auburn, New York prison.

While in jail, the "prison professor" Legere received hundreds of labor and socialist magazines and books which he used as teaching tools. "In six months we had made the prison school a center of revolutionary socialist and industrial union propaganda," Legere wrote. "I found it easy to interest the prisoners in socialism," he continued. "In fact, most of the prisoners there for crimes against property are men who, driven to rebel against the rigors of capitalist exploitation, naturally turn to burglary." Legere's teaching helped these men understand that there were more effective ways to challenge the system than by breaking and entering.

The prison warden was not the biggest obstacle to Legere's organizing. Rather, it was Thomas Mott Osborne, derisively called "the millionaire reformer" by the Wobbly. "Auburn prison was his plaything," Legere charged. Osborne created within the facility a "Mutual Welfare League" which purported to teach democracy and self-reliance to the inmates. Legere and his dedicated students ran an aggressive election campaign for League office, which prompted Osborne to attempt to transfer the instigator out of Auburn. Legere later analyzed his imprisonment in the *International Socialist Review*, exposing conditions he said were designed to break the inmates' spirits. He would also write on prison reform in *The New Republic* with the ironic title "Prisons as Pleasure Resorts."

After his jail term, Legere briefly promoted speaking engagements for James Larkin and shared the stage with the famous Irish trade union leader on at least one occasion. His relationship with Matilda Rabinowitz ended. She became pregnant and insisted on having their child alone.

In Canada Legere toured with an acting company and was once again thrown in jail. This time the "crime" was wearing an IWW pin on his coat. The authorities kicked him out of the country. Legere's time in Canada, however, exposed him to the development of the One Big Union (OBU, not to be confused with the IWW's plan for "one big union"). He put all his energy into the Canadian union's formation. "The IWW had bitten off more than it could chew," Legere reflected. The union had "theorized too much [and] had undertaken a much more pretentious thing than it was possible to accomplish."

In 1922 he was back in Lawrence, organizing mill workers under the OBU banner. A number of cotton mills in Rhode Island and Massachusetts had instituted a 20% wage cut in March. While the Lawrence bosses hesitated at first, they soon announced the drastic cut as well. This triggered Legere's reappearance in the city to organize a massive strike. In keeping with the Bread and Roses legacy of 1912, Legere led a mass picket in front of the city's largest employer, the Pacific Mill. The owners got a court injunction against picketing, so Legere asked workers to "take a walk" with him back to the mill. Once the Pacific boss gave in and rescinded the pay cut, other area mills did as well.

Legere was active in the Sacco and Vanzetti defense committee, as was most every activist of his generation, part of a worldwide campaign to free the fish peddler and shoemaker. Falsely accused of killing a payroll guard, they were eventually executed in 1927. By 1934 Legere was living in California, helping to lead Upton Sinclair's End Poverty in California (EPIC) movement and working as an actor with the United Labor Radio Campaign.

Decades before the Chinese leader Mao Zedong wrote that "revolution is not a tea party," Legere spoke to Willimantic mill workers and warned them that "this fight for the uplifting of humanity is no pink teas engagement or afternoon party." Ben Legere, whom historian Dexter Arnold dubbed "a long distance runner on the left," died on January 29, 1972 having carried on that fight all his life.

Afterward:
Beautiful Radiant Things

*The end in view is well worth striving for, but in the struggle
itself lies the happiness of the fighter.*
— A.S. Embree

It starts with your heart and radiates out.
— Cesar Chavez

In these accounts, the harshness of workers' lives is brought into sharp focus with each campaign. Too often, even the workers' victories come with great sacrifices. But while finishing this book, I was reminded that those hard facts are only part of a bigger picture.

Women and men engage in workplace battles despite long odds because they want bread, but also because they want roses. They want the opportunity to enjoy their lives and families, and to gain the respect they deserve for the work they do. Their battles remind me what I have tried to incorporate in my own union organizing over the past 35 years: our goal is to increase workers' power, and we must win real victories that improve peoples' lives, but we should *enjoy* the struggle as well.

We can't know everything that these early 20th century workers thought and felt, since there are few first-hand accounts. And yet small details shine through, glimpses of the joy that can be found even in difficult times.

Recall the scene of young Hartford couples packing the sidewalk, dressed in their Sunday best, in front of the IWW dance hall; the Mechanicsville children, able for the first time to attend the circus, thanks to the generosity of strike supporters; the relief and pride when poverty-stricken workers win their strike at the Quidnick Mill in Willimantic; the thrill of hearing the stirring words of great orators like Debs, Gurley Flynn, or Connolly in a Hartford hall; listening to Steve Kaminsky sing union songs from inside a police wagon while being taken to a Waterbury jail.

As Emma Goldman, who understood the Wobbly spirit, wrote: "I want freedom, the right to self-expression, everybody's right to beautiful, radiant things." Here's to dancing at *that* revolution.

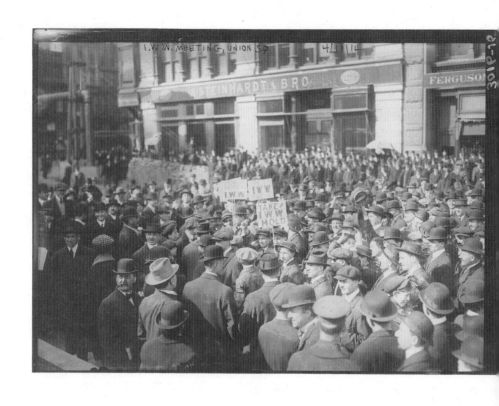

Notes

Preamble of the Industrial Workers of the World

The working class and the employing class have nothing in common. There can be no peace so long as hunger and want are found among millions of working people and the few, who make up the employing class, have all the good things of life.

Between these two classes a struggle must go on until the workers of the world organize as a class, take possession of the earth and the machinery of production, and abolish the wage system.

We find that the centering of the management of industries into fewer and fewer hands makes the trade unions unable to cope with the ever growing power of the employing class. The trade unions foster a state of affairs which allows one set of workers to be pitted against another set of workers in the same industry, thereby helping defeat one another in wage wars. Moreover, the trade unions aid the employing class to mislead the workers into the belief that the working class have interests in common with their employers.

These conditions can be changed and the interest of the working class upheld only by an organization formed in such a way that all its members in any one industry, or in all industries, if necessary, cease work whenever a strike or lockout is on in any department thereof, thus making an injury to one an injury to all.

Instead of the conservative motto, "A fair day's wages for a fair day's work," we must inscribe on our banner the revolutionary watchword, "Abolition of the wage system."

It is the historic mission of the working class to do away with capitalism. The army of production must be organized, not only for the every day struggle with capitalists, but also to carry on production when capitalism shall have been overthrown. By organizing industrially we are forming the structure of the new society within the shell of the old.

How God Blesses This Weaver's House *by Matilda Rabinowitz*

"It is 4:30 of a dark, raw December morning. The fire which Mrs. Luther Lee Jackson built in the grate after supper, the night before, has burnt out hours ago. The ashes of it are being blown about the room by the draughts which come in from the cracks in the floor, the doors, and the loose, rattling window sashes. The room is cold and bare, but for two beds, one of iron, painted in some dark color, and the other an old wooden one, and a commode to match it. A rusty lantern with a smoky, broken chimney, is flickering on the mantel above the fire-place. In one of the beds are Luther Lee Jackson, weaver in the Branwood cotton mill, and his better and leaner half, a spinner in that same mill. In the other bed the three Jackson children are huddled together under a heap of old patchwork quilts, which make up in weight what they lack in warmth. There are no sheets on either of the beds; old gray blankets are spread over the coarse straw mattress, and the pillows have no covers.

"Mrs. Jackson was awake the biggest part of the night, partly from cold, and partly because, as she puts it herself, 'Ah done been havin' the asthma so bad them last six years, that nary a wink can ah sleep some of the nights.' She is now wide awake, and lies still as if listening for something.

"A low, muffled blowing is heard. It increases in volume, as others coming from many directions are added to it, until it becomes an unmuffled fog horn, blowing plaintively through the dark, wretched mill village. This is called the 'wake whistle' among the mill workers. The legend runs that this early morning 'wake' originated with the idea that the mill hands were too poor to buy alarm clocks and were apt to oversleep.

"Mrs. Jackson drags herself out of the bed and begins pulling up her shoes; her stockings she seldom removes at night, during the winter.

"'Law' me, Law' me, them feet o' mine sure done swell some. Ah cain't get my shoes on nohow,' she murmurs with a sigh.

"The whistles keep up their uncanny blowing. Mrs. Jackson finally succeeds in tying the laces about her swollen ankles and begins to call: 'Luther, Jennings, Madge, ain't ye all heerd the wake? Ah spec' ye all better be a helpin' me with the fire, or ah cain't get breakfas' nohow. The pine's wet, Ah do know, with this rough weather, and there ain't but a bit a' kerosene oil in the tin.' Again telling the family to make haste and get up, she shuffles out of the room.

"Luther and Jennings and Madge begin to dress. Madge always dresses under cover. She is shivering in her little cotton chemise, her chest hollow and shoulder blades protruding, and she has all the ear marks of an overworked and underfed child.

"Madge, Ah reck'n you better run roun' to Mrs. Grant's and ask to borrow some oil fer to put on the pine; it's wet and green, and won't burn, nohow,' she says, and she goes out, the whole family now following.

"The lamp throws a yellow light around the room. The walls are unplastered and entirely bare but for some rusty nails, with some clothing hung upon them. Over one of the doors is a print of pink and blue coloring with 'God Bless Our Home' on it.

"A half an hour later the family sits down to breakfast. It consists of a tin of biscuits, a few slices of thick, cheap bacon, and some dark brown concoction which the Jacksons call coffee. They eat without speaking to one another, each, as it seems, trying to get through with the food before the other. The whistles are blowing again. It is 5:30 and the Jacksons hurry to the mill.

"It is 12 o'clock. The mill which has hours before swallowed hundreds of men, women, and children, has thrown open its doors to let them out. They hurry out and down the hill toward their houses which are scattered around the mill in long, uneven rows, the streets about them crooked and muddy. The houses are all of the same style and with hardly a foundation to stand on, low-roofed and painted gray. What sorry houses and what sad looking inhabitants.

"Mrs. Jackson gets home a little before the rest of the family. Married women have that privilege in mill. Madge, who is also a spinner, can watch her mother's 'sides' until the whistle blows and the power is shut off. In the meantime Mrs. Jackson warms up some beans which are left over from the night before, fries up some slices of bacon, and that with some biscuits from the morning meal, constitutes the family dinner. They hurry through it in a few minutes and rush to the mill again.

"They must hurry. The machinery is started up at 12:30. There is danger of warps getting caught; threads may break, harnesses slip off and there will be fines to pay for imperfect work, and time lost in repairs, and a call down from the overseer. So hurry they must. Jennings, who is only twelve, sometimes stops to play, picking up stones and then throwing them from him, or carving into a piece of wood with his knife; but his sister always calls back to him and tells him someone will get his 'spools,' and he drops his play and runs to the mill.

"All day—for twelve long hours the weaver sweats at his loom. The heat and humidity of the weave-room is unbearable. He runs from twenty-four to thirty looms; as he sometimes puts it 'an acre of looms.' He weaves, weaves, weaves, endlessly, hopelessly. His mind is blank. He doesn't; he cannot think. He can only weave. Before him runs the white cloth—hundreds of yards, thousands of yards, millions of yards. So many years—twenty-nine years—he has been seeing white cloth run before his eyes. Nothing but white cloth. His life is one stretch of white cloth. He walks up and down before his looms like a slave in a treadmill. And all around are other slaves, all walking up and down before their looms; all sweating, all watching while white cloth runs before their eyes, all weaving, weaving endlessly, hopelessly.

"All day—for twelve long hours, his wife and daughter watch the spinning frames. Up and down they go with heavy limbs and tired eyes. Bobbins whirl, spindles fly, threads break—so many threads—the arms get so tired from reaching up and tying them together. A thousand spindles for one pair of eyes to watch! Madge thought she never would get used to tying so many threads. She used to come to her mother and cry that too many threads were breaking. Not so many break now, but the reaching up is so hard. Something inside of her seems to stretch and ache, and ache. And when the day is over she is so tired, she just drags herself. And sometimes in her sleep, she cries out in pain, and reaches out her hands as if to tie threads that break. She keeps on tying threads, and watching spindles fly, and bobbins whirl, and spinning-spinning-spinning her young life and laughter and joy into fine white thread.

"The night is cold, and there is a fire in the small, open grate in the Jackson home. Luther sits before the fire smoking his pipe and spitting upon the hot coals every few seconds. Madge and her mother are cleaning up, and washing up some dishes for the next twenty-four hours. The two boys are already asleep—Jennings goes to bed as soon as he has had his beans and corn bread and molasses and coffee. But in the morning he is the hardest to wake, his mother says. She says he is 'delicate' and fears the mill 'is a' hurtin' him'.

"When Mrs. Jackson and Madge come to the fire, after their tasks, they find Luther Lee asleep in the chair with his bare feet on the grate. They both take their shoes off and hold their feet before the fire, talking about the work in the mill. Every night they warm their feet and talk about the work in the mill, or about the mill girls; who got married and who died; or about the new farm help that is ' a'comin' and a'comin' and making so many spare hands.' The channel of conversation while they sit and warm their feet.

"A few last coals are still glowing in the grate. The lantern is again smoking on the mantel, the chairs around the fire place are deserted and all is quiet. Only the snoring of Luther Lee is heard. The moon shines through an uncurtained window, and in its light can be read the words over the door—'God Bless Our Home'."

Organizers & Allies of the IWW in Connecticut, 1905-1919

1905 — James Lee, Joe Campbell, Samuel Stodell

1906 — August Buetter

1907 — J.T. Vaughn, Frank Bohn, Elizabeth Gurley Flynn, Carlo Tresca, Samuel French, Louis Basky

1908 — Bill Haywood, Luella Twining

1911 — Robert M. Lackey, Joseph L. Ryan, Ben Legere

1912 — Fred Ellery, Delegate Powers, Loigeo, Grover H. Perry, Ben Legere, Jan Smit, Shykrie Swyden, John Buzskelzc, Cyrille De Tollenaere, Arthur Jacobs, Arthur Payette, Laura Marcotte, Carlo Amoto, Raimondo Fazio, Walter Eggeman, Meyer Friedkin, John Bush, Donato Di Donato, Jean Spielman, Guido Giannini, Yates, Pollock, Michael Ossip, J.T. Bienkowski, Jean E. Spielman, Edmono Rossino, Antone Mazzatello, Benjamin L. Legere, Walter Eggeman, Robert M. Lackey

1913 — Rudolph Katz, Arturo Giovannitti, Emma Goldman, Carlo Tresca, Helen Keller, Alexander Schidlowski, Thomas F. Connolly, John Smelstorious, Waclaw Chotkowski, M.K. Bolis, Stanley Bayer, J. Mazeika, Adam Kulas, R. Gley, Michael Dumas, Matilda Rabinowitz

1914 — Michael Dumas, Arturo Giovannitti, Ernest Mohl

1915 — Louis Nelson, Herman Klevens

1916 — Joe Ettor, Elizabeth Gurley Flynn, Joe Bonish

1917 — Angelo Del Grosso

1919 — Carlo Tresca, Steve Kaminsky, Mark Zeitlin, Paul Matecky, Alex Pashug, Alexander Chernoff, Peter Kraskowsky, Sam "Bernow" Bernowsky, Michael Rosenberg, Harry Nelson

Thanks

Special thanks go to my fellow workers and friends: Nancy Chance, Peter Kellman, Mims Butterworth, and in particular, Dexter Arnold.

Also, many thanks to Jeremy Brecher, Sonny San Juan, Delia Aguilar, Bernardo McLaughlin, Cele Bucki, Paul Wessel, John Del Vecchio, and John Murphy.

Without their feedback, encouragement, and friendship, this book would still be listed under the heading of "coulda, woulda, shoulda."

Credits

The front and back cover are the work of the very talented peoples' artist Christian Murray. Photo of Steve courtesy of the intrepid Nick Lacy.

Inspiration

I would never have known that there is another history out there—one that documents our struggle for social and economic justice—had it not been for the works of the following historians: Herbert Aptheker, Howard Zinn, Philip Foner, Jeremy Brecher, Richard Moyer and Herbert Morais, and Harvey Wasserman. Also, thanks to my teacher and mentor Paul Boccaccio.

Find Out More

The IWW is alive and kicking! Visit their web site, buy their newspaper, join the ranks at www.iww.org.

Red Sun Press printed this book. Their motto is "printing for peace and justice since 1973." Red Sun, located in Jamaica Plain, Massachusetts, is a democratically controlled, environmentally sustainable, UAW shop.

Steve's website, **ShoeleatherHistoryProject.com,** has lots more stories from the grassroots. He is a member of the IWW and the National Writers Union (www.nwu.org)

Biography

Steve Thornton is a retired organizer with the largest healthcare workers union in Connecticut, District 1199/SEIU, as well as with the Greater Hartford Labor Council. He is also on the national steering committee of US Labor Against the War (USLAW), of which District 1199 was a founding member in 2003. Steve has spent his adult life as an activist and organizer. In high school and college he organized against racism and the Vietnam War and published in the underground press.

In Hartford, Connecticut, where he has lived since 1973, Steve began as a housing rights activist, organizing tenants being displaced by corporate redevelopment, and homeless men into a direct action group. From 1987 to 1993 he helped create and played a key role in People For Change, a third party that successfully elected City Council members around a pro-union, LGBT-friendly, populist platform.

Steve previously worked with the International Ladies Garment Workers Union (now UNITE HERE), organizing and leading strikes primarily with people of color in small manufacturing and the textile industry. His union work began as an elected steward while employed as a day care teacher, where he ran for and won the position of Executive Vice President of AFSCME Local 1716. He was later hired as an organizer for the union of community college faculty and professionals, where he built a statewide lobbying effort that increased funding for working people, and where he organized mass student rallies.

Steve has continued to work with various groups for social, economic, and environmental justice, including the Clamshell Alliance, Anti-Racism Coalition of Connecticut, Irish Northern Aid and the War Resisters League.

Over the past thirty-five years he has trained hundreds of activists in nonviolent direct action in New England, Washington D.C. and Georgia, and more than 2,000 healthcare workers as rank and file leaders. He has helped build solidarity connections with working peoples' struggles in Havana, Belfast, Managua, Vicenza, and Oslo. Steve's work as a local activist is featured in the new book *Social Movements and Activists in the USA* by Stephen Valocchi.

Sources

INTRODUCTION
Public Hearings Before the Joint Standing
  Committee on Military Affairs,
General Assembly of the State of Connecticut, January Session, 1905
Domesticating the Street, Peter C. Baldwin
1999, Ohio University Press
Hartford Times, June 27, 1905
"SDS: Why Now (Again)?", Paul Buhle, MRzine,
  Monthly Review Foundation, January 15, 2006
Hine, Lewis photographs, 102-LH-488, 523148; 102-LH-
  533, 523155 research.archives.gov/description/523064

WHY WOULD WORKERS JOIN THE IWW?
Hartford Courant, August 6, 1895, February 16,
  1906, April 4, 1906, February 17, 1913
Hartford Times, July 7, 1904 February 23, 1912
New York Times, February 23, 1906, May 30, 1912
Waterbury American April 16, 1913
Bridgeport Evening Farmer, October 13, 1912
New Haven Evening Register, March 8, 1912, May 11, 1912
Willimantic Chronicle, November 15, 1912

GET MRS. PARSONS TO STOP TALKING
Lucy Parsons, American Revolutionary, Carolyn Asbaugh,
  Charles H. Kerr Publishing Company 1976
New Haven Morning News, November 1, 1886
New Haven Evening Register, October 31, 1886
Morning Journal and Courier, November 1, 1886
Lucy Parsons Portrait hdl.handle.net/2451/27776

FIRST STIRRINGS
Hartford Evening Post, September 15, 16, 1905
Hartford Courant, September 16 , 30, 1905
Washington Post, March 7—15, 1905
I use the term Wobbly throughout, even though the nickname
  was not coined until around 1913. For the possible origin of
  the name see Archie Green's essay in Wobblies, Pile Butts,
  and Other Heroes, 1993, University of Illinois Press
Bridgeport Evening Farmer, May-August 1907
The Rebel Girl An Autobiography, My First Life (1906-1926),
  Elizabeth Gurley Flynn, International Publishers, 1982
The Industrial Workers of the World: Its First 100 Years, Fred
  Thompson and Jon Bekken, 2006, IWW publishers
Labor History, Fall, 1989, Vol. 30 No 4 "Summer Lightning
  1907: The Wobblies in Bridgeport," Robert J. Embardo
Bridgeport's Socialist New Deal, Cecelia Bucki,
  University of Illinois Press, 2001
Bridgeport Evening Post, May 16—August 20, 1907
History of the Labor Movement in the United States,
  Volume 4, The Industrial Workers of the World, 1905-
  1917, Philip S. Foner, International Publishers (1973)
Thanks to the Bridgeport Public library for AT & S Factory photo
Bain Collection Photos - hdl.loc.gov/loc.pnp/pp.ggbain
  Lawrence strike meeting, New York. LC-DIG-ggbain-10184;
  Elizabeth Gurley Flynn (Mrs. J.A. Jones), 1890-
  1964, full-length portrait, standing, facing front, in
  public speaking posture LC-USZ62-48852;
  Guarding approach to mills, Lawrence,
  Mass. LC-DIG-ggbain-10151;
  I.W.W. Meeting -- Union Sq. LC-DIG-ggbain-15711;
  Crowd of strikers menacing strike-breakers,
  Lawrence, LC-DIG-ggbain-10150

UNDESIRABLE CITIZEN
Hartford Daily Courant, June 20, 1908
Hartford Evening Post, 1908: April 7—28; May 15; June 18, 20
Hartford Times, June 20, 1908

Hartford Courant, March 11, 1907
An Encyclopedia of American History, Howard L.
  Hurvitz, Washington Square Press, March 1970
Red November Black November, Salvatore Salerno,
  State University of New York Press, 197

RED EMMA
Living My Life, Volume One by Emma Goldman,
  Dover Publications, Inc. 1970

DEBS, PROPHET OF SOCIALISM
Hartford Courant, June 4, 1910
Hartford Times, June 4, 1910
The Fall of the House of Labor, David Montgomery,
  Cambridge University Press, 1995
International Socialist Review, February, 1918, as quoted
  in Debs Speaks, Pathfinder Press, 1996, Indiana State
  Library, Victor L. Greenwood letters to Debs, 1921

BROTHERHOOD OF MACHINISTS
Bridgeport Evening Farmer, March 10—21, 1911,
Bridgeport Post, April 5, 8, 1911
International Socialist Review, November 1912

THE BAD ELEMENT IN TOWN
Hartford Courant, May 25, 28; June 6, 1912
Norwich Bulletin, April 11-22 1912, May 25-30 1912; June 1- 28, 1912
The Penny Press, May 25; June 5, 1912
Putnam Patriot, April 12, 19; May 31; June 14—28; July 5, 1912
Bridgeport Evening Farmer, April 11, 1912

WILDFIRE IN THREAD CITY
Norwich Bulletin, April 23—30, 1912
Putnam Patriot, May 3, 1912
Willimantic Chronicle, May, 1912
Hood, Sam, 1934, Home and Away Photo: 4368, acms.sl.nsw.gov.au

THE FORTY-INCH YARD
Penny Press, May 7-June 22, 1912
Middletown Sun, May-June 1912
Hartford Courant, May-June 1912
Hartford Times, May-June 1912
New York Times, June 6, 1912

THE RED MENACE
The Nation, June 12, 1920, February 7, 1920

THE BOSS GETS WHAT HE PAYS FOR
Norwalk Hour, 1913: April 16—29; May 3, 27; June 10—17
Testimony, Senate Committee on Finance, March 17, 1913

LOOKING THE WORLD STRAIGHT IN THE EYE
Helen Keller, by Leslie Garrett, DK Publishing, Inc. 2004
New York Call, November 13, 1912, January 1913
Hartford Courant, April 1, 2, 5, May 20, 1913
Justice, October, 1913
New York Tribune, January 3, 1916
Helen Keller's FBI File, www.foia.fbi.gov/foiaindex/hellenkeller.htm

THE RIOT THAT WASN'T
Hartford Courant, May 19, 1913
Waterbury American, May 19, 1913

DAMAGE CONTROL
Hartford Courant, January 24, 1914
www.iww.org/culture/library/sabotage/
www.iww.org/organize/strategy/Sabotage2.shtml

BLACK WORKERS AND THE IWW
Hartford Courant, February 13, 1919
New London Day, November 15, 1919
Hartford Daily Times, August 30, 1904, March 26, 1918
Hartford Daily Courant, March 11, 1918
Hartford Times, January 16, 1945
Hartford Courant, September 24, 1908
Hartford Times, May 6, 1940

BREAD AND ROSES
Bridgeport Evening Farmer, February 22, 23, 26, 1912
Hartford Times, February 22, 1912

THE HIGH COSTS OF ORGANIZING
Bristol Press, April 7, 17, 18, 19, 21, 25, 1917, May 2, 4, 5, 14, 17, 1917
Hartford Courant, April 18, May 4, 1917

IWW VS. IWW
The Wobblies, The Story of the IWW and Syndicalism in the
    United States, Patrick Renshaw, Ivan R. Dee publishers, 1967
The IWW, A Study in American Syndicalism, Paul
    F. Brissenden, Russell & Russell, Inc., 1919
Strike!, Jeremy Brecher, 1972, Straight Arrow Books
New Haven Evening Register, November 26, 1900
Hartford Times, May 3, September 2, 17, 1916
Hartford Courant, February 26, 1906
Hartford Courant, April 1, 1912

A NEW SPECIES OF PLAGUE
Hartford Daily Times, May 30, 1912 and March 23, 1918
Norwich Bulletin, May 4, 1912
New Haven Evening Register, January 25, 1919
History, Memory, and the City: Life Stories of Growing Up in
    Hartford, Connecticut During the Great Depression, Steve
    Valocchi, Connecticut History, Volume 4 Number 1, Spring 202
Hartford Courant, May 26, 1913, July 2, 1913,
    August 21, 1913, March 9, 1914
Meriden Daily Journal, May 13, 1913
New Haven Evening Register, March 19, 1914

THE MILLIONAIRE SOCIALIST
Proceedings of the First Convention of the Industrial Workers
    of the World, New York Labor News Company, 1905
Hartford Courant, January 27, May 31, October 2, November 27, 1912
Who's Who in New England 1916, A.N Marquis & Company
International Socialist Review, August, 1912
We Shall Be All, Melvyn Dubofsky, 1969,
    Quadrangle/New York Times Books
The American Lamonts, by Jim Sleeper, New
    York Times, October 15, 2006
Il Proletario, August 17, 1912

NO ANARCHISTS ON BOARD
Almanac of American History, Arthur M. Schlesinger
    Jr., editor, Brompton Books Corporation, 1993
SS Caronia manifest list, October 30, 1910

MISTAKEN IDENTITY
Battling for American Labor, Howard Kimmeldorf,
    University of California Press
New Haven Times Leader, January 11 and 13, 191_
The IWW: A Study in American Syndicalism, Paul
    F. Brissenden, Russell & Russell, Inc. 1919
New Haven Morning Journal Courier January 25, 1913
Corriere del Connecticut, January 18, 1913
Bridgeport Evening Farmer, September 2, 1915

TAKE AWAY THEIR GUNS AND GIVE THEM SHOVELS
New Haven Morning Journal Courier, January 25, 1913

THE DANGEROUS PROPOSITION
The Evening Sentinel (Ansonia), March 24—29, April 5—22, 1913
Solidarity, November 29, 1913, February 14, 1914
Bridgeport Evening Farmer, December 29—31, 1913;
    January 2—31, 1914; February 2—4, 1914
Bridgeport Telegram, January 5, 1914
Hartford Courant, February 14, 1914

HOW GOD BLESSES THIS WEAVER'S HOUSE
Matilda Robbins: A Woman's Life in the Labor Movement, 1900-1920
Joyce Shaw Peterson, Labor History, Volume
    34, Issue 1 Winter 1993 , pages 33 – 56
Greenville "Lint-heads" http://facweb.furman.
    edu/~benson/h41tg2.html
Child Labor, An American History, Hugh
    D. Hinman, M.E. Sharpe, 2002
Waterbury Herald, February 14, 1915

ANONYMOUS BUT NOT FORGOTTEN
Hartford Courant May 17, 1915, August 25, 1915, July 14, 1915,
    October 17, 1915, November 13, 1915, June 10, 1917, June 5, 1918,
    September 27, 1917, April 10, 1919, June 26, 1919, July 10, 17, 1919
Evening Sentinel, September 26, 27, 1918, February 24, 1919

THEY EVIDENTLY HAVE NO LEADER
Waterbury American February 22, 23, 1916
Waterbury Republican February 20, 21, 23, 24, 25, 26, 27 1916
Waterbury Evening Democrat February 21, 22, 23, 24, 25 1916
Hartford Courant February 19, 20, 22, 1916
Bridgeport Evening Farmer, February 21, 1916

WE ARE NOT DOGS
Norwich Bulletin, May-June 1913
New London Day, May-June 1913

LABOR'S UNTOLD STORY
Hartford Courant March 4-20, 1919
Hartford Times March 3, 6, 7, 10, 11, 1919
Dangerous Lawlessness: The Murder of Frank Little
Bridgeport Evening Farmer, August 2, 1917
Frank Little/Victim of Anaconda Copper Co. Thugs. Died
    Aug 1, 1917 Butte Mont, University of Washington

YOUNG SEEDS OF SEDITION
Hartford Courant, March 21, 1919

SONGS TO FAN THE FLAMES OF DISCONTENT
Waterbury Republican, June 18-25, 1919
Waterbury American, June 25-28, July 5, 1919
Connecticut Labor Press, June 28, July 5, 1919
Hartford Courant, March 10, 1919

LIKE AN OAK TREE
All the Right Enemies, The Life and Murder of Carlo
    Tresca, Dorothy Gallagher, Penguin Books, 1988
http://www.harvardsquarelibrary.org/unitarians/baldwin.html
FBI files Number 2 and 3 on Carlo Tresca released under FOIA,
    http://foia.fbi.gov/tresca/tresca2.pdf (no longer available on line)
Hartford Daily Courant, Monday, November 3, 1919
Hartford Post, November 3, 1919

THE RED LAWS IN CONNECTICUT, 1919
Connecticut General Statutes, 1919, pages
    2703, 2829-2830, 2842, 2872